Extinguishin

FEAR

30 Devotions to Battle
Fear and Anxiety

A Devotable Compilation Project

Extinguishing the Spirit of Fear
30 Devotions to Battle Fear and Anxiety

Devotable is a brand trying to reach the world with the Gospel of Jesus Christ.

We try to do three things through our platform. First, we want to encourage believers daily with insightful and powerful devotions. Second, we try to reach the lost through the power of daily scripture and devotion reading. Lastly, we spread the word of God around the world with technology.

In everything we do, this is our passion and mission. If you want to learn more about us, connect with us, or be a part of our awesome movement, visit our website at

https://devotableapp.com

Table of Contents

FEAR

We live in a time when fear and anxiety are the status quo.

We fear what is awaiting us with every new day. We're anxious to find a place where we feel we belong, like we're accepted. We stay awake at night thinking of all the work we've yet to finish, and we turn on the news only to find more reasons to lose sleep.

Another shooting.

Another contentious election.

Another untimely death.

Another reason to fear and let anxiety blow the sails of our souls.

What are we to do?

A brief Google search offers an abundance of cures. Our problem is we're unhealthy, so here's a 6-week exercise program with guaranteed results. Look at all the reviews, surely this will do it! Or maybe that's not it, what you need is to level up your game. The problem is you're using the wrong productivity system so you're behind and anxious. Buy this book and its corresponding 3-month planner. Follow along and kiss your anxiety goodbye! Actually, what you need are more Instagram followers. Once you hit 2,000 everyone will love you and you'll never be stressed again!

If only the solution to our problems were this simple. If only we could take a course and buy a book. Then all would be right in our world.

All of our Google solutions aren't entirely false. They do offer treatments. A better workout routine and healthier lifestyle will certainly help. Having a good system to stay on top of things isn't a bad idea at all. I know I couldn't stay afloat without one! And, I've no doubt hitting 2,000 Instagram followers feels good. The real problem with these solutions isn't that they're wrong or bad.

Here's the truth.

The problem is they don't go deep enough. They don't bring us to the root of our anxiety. It's like slapping a band aid on a flesh wound; they bring only marginal healing.

What's needed is to go deeper because when you get down to the root, when you dig through the fog of anxious despair, you find there's another reality, another dimension hardly spoken of. This is the dimension of the soul.

We are not only flesh and bones but also souls. Souls who are crafted by divine fingers for something more than what this world has to offer. Something deeper than a simple Google search can cure. Something which is only found in a kingdom which is foreign to this world — the kingdom of God.

In this kingdom we find promises which are kept, words which will never perish, and a God who has a personal history with anxiety and fear. A God who took on human flesh to free us from our anxious plight.

A God who entered into our human longings and anxious fears. A God who died to set us free and rose again to give us life.

This life cannot be found anywhere else and this freedom cannot be lost.

The pages that follow are an invitation. They invite you to look at your anxiety and fear in the deepest levels; to go beyond what's on the surface and get to your heart. At its core, this is an invitation to believe Jesus' words to His disciples are words to you as well. "Peace I leave with you. My peace I give to you. I do not give to you as the world gives. Don't let your heart be troubled or fearful" (John 14:27).

If you keep looking, you'll find an endless supply of reasons for your heart to be troubled. If you look to the Man Christians call Messiah, you'll find an endless supply of reasons for your heart to have peace. In the process, you'll find peace isn't a thing to be had but a God to hold onto.

What you'll find in these pages isn't a quick fix or a one size fits all solution. No. You might not find anything, in fact. Or you may just find your whole being re-oriented at your deepest level.

You may find that peace you've always been looking for.
    You may find yourself with Jesus of Nazareth.
    Who knows?
    If fear and anxiety are things you struggle with, let's walk this path together and find help.

by JD Tyler

HOW TO USE THIS DEVOTIONAL

Each day starts with a devotional. Read the devotional and accompanying Scripture to learn more about fear and how it affects your life.

Each day of the week, there is a question relating to that daily devotion. These questions are designed to help you go deeper into that daily devotion, exploring more about the topic. They also encourage dialogue exploring how the Bible teaches us to behave and respond to those subjects.

Use those questions to help guide you in self-reflection, biblical application, and spiritual growth.

As you continue with the journal, you'll be able to look back at the previous pages and see how things you were once praying about have been fulfilled. You'll get a better sense of how God is working through your life and how He is answering your prayers.

Often we pray for something and forget about it several weeks down the road. Journaling these things helps us remember just how good God is to always answer our prayers.

To obtain a copy of the journaling pages for free, please go to https://devotableapp.com/fearjournalpages/

You can download a printable version of the devotional journal pages and keep up just like the physical book.

DAY 1

Peace from Negative Thoughts and Anxiety

"Don't worry about anything, but in everything, through prayer and petition with thanksgiving, present your requests to God" Philippians 4:6

Have you ever struggled with negative thoughts or anxiety? I sure have. I fixate on a problem and then it becomes a broken record in my head. Soon, that negative thing is all I can think about. I notice my mood changes. I start to feel fearful, distrusting, vulnerable, and unsafe. I walk in doom instead of the joy God has for me.

Thankfully, God is patient and persistent. When there is a small break in the storm that's formed in my mind, His voice softly breaks through, "Daughter, those thoughts and voices are not from me. You are being attacked!" It's as if a light bulb has turned on, illuminating the darkest corners of my mind, filling it with the truth. With this new knowledge, I can fight the enemy — the REAL enemy — who is Satan. I pray, rebuking him and demanding that he leave me and my mind alone. The anxious, dark, gloomy thoughts instantly cease. I'm able to see the situation clearly. It's amazing how fast peace will come when

we allow the light to expose the dark.

I'm in a season of learning how much your thoughts can dictate your actions. Everything we do starts with a thought. If I decide something is difficult before I even begin, I will talk myself out of doing what I am supposed to do. This leads to procrastination, which leads to more stress and negative thoughts. It's a vicious cycle. Yet it's a cycle I often find myself caught up in. Can you relate?

Friends, we are not supposed to live a life riddled with anxiety or negative thoughts. God wants us to have peace. It is so important to take every thought captive and measure them up to God's truth. If you are like me, you like direction or steps you need to take to be successful.

Philippians 4:6-7 gives you an excellent guide to follow if you deal with anxiety. "Don't worry about anything, but in everything, through prayer and petition with thanksgiving, present your requests to God. And the peace of God, which surpasses all understanding, will guard your hearts and minds in Christ Jesus."

For me, anxiety starts when I feel like I have to be in control and have all the answers. Guys, we are so blessed to have a God who is asking to carry all of that stuff for us. When you are feeling anxious about anything, stop and take some time to be alone with

DAY 1

God. I've done it myself and have found so much peace.

Next, when those negative thoughts like to pop up, use Philippians 4:8 as your guide. Ask yourself, "Finally brothers and sisters, whatever is true, whatever is honorable, whatever is just, whatever is pure, whatever is lovely, whatever is commendable — if there is any moral excellence and if there is anything praiseworthy — dwell on these things." This is something I constantly have to work on. I wish it was an overnight fix, but it takes time and patience. Measure your thoughts to Philippians 4:8. If they don't match up, throw those thoughts out!

When you find yourself struggling with negative thoughts and anxiety, reflect back on Philippians 4:6-8. Know that you can come to God with anything and everything. He will show you the truth and help you throw out anything that threatens to take your peace.

Written By Alexis Newlin

DAY 1
QUESTIONS

What steps can you take to combat anxiety whenever it starts to creep into your thought life?

Today I praise God for...

Today I am confessing...

Today I am praying for...

PRAYER

God, my head knows I can come to you with any problem I might be tackling, but sometimes my heart is a little slower. Bring peace and light to my mind, revealing what is You and what is of this world. Help me to throw out anything that robs me of Your peace. Amen.

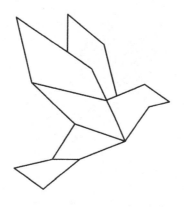

If the Lord be with us, we have no cause of fear. His eye is upon us, His arm over us, His ear open to our prayer - His grace sufficient, His promise unchangeable.

-John Newton

DAY 2

Keeping the Faith in Time of Crisis

"The Lord is my light and my salvation—whom should I fear? The Lord is the stronghold of my life—whom should I dread?" Psalm 27:1

How can we keep the faith in a time of crisis? Sometimes the storm takes us completely by surprise: the bad report, the betrayal of a friend, the crisis at work, the suffering of a loved one. From one second to another we are transferred to another reality sweeping through our souls and bodies with waves of fear and anxiety. Our boats are rocking on a raging sea. We find it difficult to concentrate, to pray, to think clearly, and to stay firm in faith in a time of crisis.

The most important but difficult thing to do in times of crisis is to lift our gaze from the fear and to focus our attention on the Lord. The more we focus on the Lord, on His character, and on His promises, the more we can receive His peace and guidance. The Bible calls this having a steadfast mind, trusting in God (Isaiah 26:3). We can do this by wrapping our minds around a verse or a phrase anchoring us to a higher reality. Psalm 27 is full of such peace and hope-giving words. David speaks to his fears and anxiety proclaiming that God is his light, salvation, and

stronghold. Is this not everything we need in a time of crisis?

To stay firm in faith in a time of crisis we need to remember who God is and what He has done for us in the past. Remembering is a spiritual discipline that we need to master. The Hebrew word zakar is widely used in the Bible, mostly in the Old Testament and in the Psalms. It is translated in English with the words "remember", "remembered", or "remembrance." A few other translations include "mention", "think", and "mindful." However, zakar means not only to remember but also to think or pay attention to.

Remembering God means to acknowledge, to focus on, to consider, to take into account, to meditate on, not to forget who He is, what He has done, and what He has promised to do. This discipline helps us stay connected with the truth and the higher reality of His presence and love.

We practice focusing on God by:
- engaging in prayer and praise
- calling on His name
- reflecting and talking about what He has done for us in the past
- boasting in His name
- singing and choosing to rejoice despite the circumstances.

God invites us to search and find our joy, shelter, and peace

DAY 2

in Him during the storm. He is the one who keeps us safe in times of crisis: "For he will conceal me in his shelter in the day of adversity; he will hide me under the cover of his tent; he will set me high on a rock" (Psalm 27:5). He is also a God, who remembers – His covenant, His promises, all our sorrows and tears, our deepest desires and needs. He is a God, who remembers us every day choosing in Christ to give us abundant life and eternal blessings.

Sharing our troubles with our brothers and sisters and allowing them to meet our needs is also part of God's provision in a time of crisis. We don't live in a vacuum; God has provided for us a family to get support and encouragement.

It is helpful to think of ourselves as soldiers. When the soldiers are not actively engaged on the battlefield, they are on the training field, practicing and honing their skills, preparing for what is to come. Every day and season are a training ground for us – learning to seek the Lord in all circumstances, to know Him more, and training our minds and souls to stay fixed on Him and His beauty. Because gazing at the beauty of the Lord is what makes us stable and strong so we can take heart and wait for Him in confidence.

Written By Hadassah Treu

DAY 2
QUESTIONS

What are some exercises you can do to train your mind and soul to trust the Lord when you're not actively engaged in battle?

_____

_____

_____

Today I praise God for...

_____

_____

Today I am confessing...

_____

_____

Today I am praying for...

_____

_____

_____

PRAYER

Dear Lord, uncertainty and chaos breed fear and anxiety. Lord, we need You. Please, fill us with the knowledge of Your will. Help us live as You want and do what pleases You. Help us produce all kinds of good deeds and grow in the knowledge of You. Most of all, make us strong with all the strength that comes from You, so that we may be able to endure everything with patience and joy. In the name of Jesus, Amen.

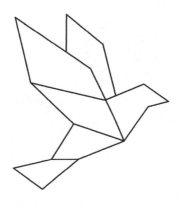

Worry is a cycle of inefficient thoughts whirling around a center of fear.

-Corrie Ten Boom

DAY 3

Is It Okay to Question God?

"I will stand at my guard post and station myself on the lookout tower. I will watch to see what he will say to me and what I should reply about my complaint" Habakkuk 2:1

Have you ever been frustrated with God? When things go wrong or when life gets too heavy to handle, I think it's human nature to ask God for answers. But how many of us are bold enough to question God? God, why did this happen to me? God, why are you letting them go through this?

There are times we may have questions about our faith or about our circumstances, but we're afraid to ask. Why do you think that is? Maybe when we were young we were told not to ask certain questions or make certain observations about the Bible or our faith. There are some faith communities where questions aren't permitted because "It's not our place to ask why." I've found this usually means there's a fear that the questions will be a threat to the powers in charge — but that's a different issue.

Questions are a natural part of life, and the Bible is filled with people asking and even demanding answers from God. And amazingly, God doesn't seem to mind.

The prophet Habakkuk demanded God answer his questions

about the oncoming destruction of Israel in his day. "I will stand at my guard post and station myself on the lookout tower. I will watch to see what he will say to me and what I should reply about my complaint" (Habakkuk 2:1). Do you hear the audacity in Habakkuk's statement? "I'm just going to stand here until you answer me, God." What do you feel when you imagine yourself talking to God with such boldness? Habakkuk's boldness paid off, because God answered his question, explaining in detail the oncoming destruction of Habakkuk's homeland because his people had blatantly disrespected God (see Habakkuk 2).

If that isn't enough evidence for you, there's no shortage of questions in the Psalms, and no shortage of anger at God either. "My God, my God, why have you abandoned me? Why are you so far from my deliverance and from my words of groaning? My God, I cry by day, but you do not answer, by night, yet I have no rest" (Psalm 22:1-2). This one verse is so powerful that Jesus even cried out the first sentence while hanging from the cross. Every Jewish person present who heard Him would have known exactly what He was saying and where it came from.

Speaking of Jesus, the disciples certainly didn't mind asking Him questions, to the point that on occasion Jesus replied, "Are you also as lacking in understanding?" (Mark 7:18). He was probably being sarcastic, but His disciples still asked for clarity

DAY 3

about Jesus' teaching when they needed it.

Asking questions is how we grow. It's when we think we have all the answers that we're in trouble. I don't think God gets angry when we ask the hard questions, because it allows Him to show us more of who He is.

If you ask the question, just be ready for the answer.

Written By Kyle Chastain

DAY 3
QUESTIONS

What questions have you been holding back from God, afraid to ask or afraid of what the answer will be?

_____
_____
_____
_____

Today I praise God for...

_____
_____
_____

Today I am confessing...

_____
_____
_____

Today I am praying for...

_____
_____
_____

PRAYER

Dearest Teacher, I don't want to be afraid to ask You questions. That's how I learn and grow. Help me to seek Your Words in Scripture to find the answers I need. Speak to my heart when the answers aren't on the written page. In Your precious and holy name, Amen.

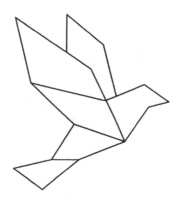

But thanks be to God, who gives us the victory through our Lord Jesus Christ! Therefore, my dear brothers and sisters, be steadfast, immovable, always excelling in the Lord's work, because you know that your labor in the Lord is not in vain.

1 Corinthians 15:57-58

DAY 4

Yielding to the Lord

"Remember my affliction and my homelessness, the wormwood and the poison. I continually remember them and have become depressed. Yet I call this to mind, and therefore I have hope: Because of the Lord's faithful love we do not perish, for his mercies never end. They are new every morning; great is your faithfulness! I say, 'The Lord is my portion, therefore I will put my hope in him'"
Lamentations 3:19-27

I am a recovering control freak. There have been countless times in my life when letting go, yielding to the Lord, was the hardest thing I ever had to do. I like everything to be in order and have a plan in place. I struggle with chaos and unorganized tasks. This internal desire to control everything slowly began to fade after I had my first child.

There is nothing like parenthood to prove that you do not have any control to begin with. During pregnancy, you worry about the little one inside of you even though you have no control over the outcome or the plan for your child's life. Yielding to the Lord begins with correctly thinking about the God who loves you and has your best interest at heart. Yielding to the Lord begins with recognizing that we can make requests to the Lord all day

long, but at the end of that day, we recognize God knows what is best in every situation.

"Remember my affliction and my homelessness, the wormwood and the poison. I continually remember them and have become depressed. Yet I call this to mind, and therefore I have hope: Because of the Lord's faithful love we do not perish, for his mercies never end. They are new every morning; great is your faithfulness! I say, 'The Lord is my portion, therefore I will put my hope in him'" (Lamentations 3:19-27).

In the verses above, we see where the writer is lamenting about all that has gone wrong. He is pouring out his heart to the Lord in prayer, sometimes begging the Lord to move in mighty ways. However, verse 21 is the game-changer. With one simple word "yet" the writer releases control, yielding to the Lord. He goes from praying with clenched hands to praying with open hands. This is where, after all his lamenting, he recognizes that his mindset must be on the hope that comes through God, not on the circumstances around him.

What does yielding to the Lord mean? When you yield to the Lord, you are giving over every ounce of control you think you may have and recognizing God is in control of the smallest details of our lives. Yielding is also recognizing that God is good and His plans are good.

DAY 4

Many times I want to be in control because I think my plans are the best ones out there. When God chooses not to answer my prayers the way this control freak thinks He should, I can become frustrated and bitter. However, yielding directs my thinking toward the right path.

We need to yield to Him in prayer. Yielding says, "Lord I have told you my plans, but I am trusting Your plans for my life because I know that Your plans are better than mine." This prayer is often the hardest when it comes to those we love. We think we know what is best for our children, our spouse, our parents, our siblings, etc. However, God created them and truly loves them far more than we ever could imagine. Yielding to the Lord's plans and purpose for them is our best option.

Yielding comes from lamenting our souls to the Lord and also recognizing that He is putting plans in motion for our lives that we cannot even begin to fathom. Yielding is also resting and trusting that God hears you and has your best interests at heart. Giving over control is difficult, but is the most rewarding choice you can make in your prayer life. Let go, rest in the "yet", and yield to what God has in store for you.

Written By Erin Woodfin

DAY 4
QUESTIONS

Recall a time in your life when the Lord's plans didn't meet your expectations but the outcome was better than you expected. How can that help you learn to trust in the Lord?

_____

_____

_____

Today I praise God for...

_____

_____

_____

Today I am confessing...

_____

_____

_____

Today I am praying for...

_____

_____

_____

PRAYER

Dear Heavenly Father, I'm opening my hands to You and acknowledging You are in control of my life. Calm my fears and help me relinquish control. Amen.

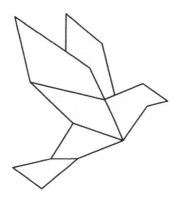

It is good to remind ourselves that the will of God comes from the heart of God and that we need not be afraid.

- Warren Wiersbe

DAY 5

Confidence in God

"Then David said to his son Solomon, "Be strong and courageous, and do the work. Don't be afraid or discouraged, for the Lord God, my God, is with you. He won't leave you or abandon you until all the work for the service of the Lord's house is finished" 1 Chronicles 28:20

How do you feel when you're asked to take on a new challenge? Are you filled with confidence, eager to give it a go, or are you hesitant, unsure whether you have what it takes?

When Solomon took over as king and prepared to build the temple, he lacked confidence, but his father, David, encouraged him to place his confidence in God, not in his own abilities. "Then David said to his son Solomon, 'Be strong and courageous, and do the work. Don't be afraid or discouraged, for the Lord God, my God, is with you. He won't leave you or abandon you until all the work for the service of the Lord's house is finished'" (1 Chronicles 28:20).

When I was asked to take on the task of leading a camp for young people a few years ago, I felt completely inadequate. This was no simple task I was being asked to do. The request came as a result of someone else pulling out, leaving a messy, complicated

situation, which I knew would present challenges. I lacked confidence in my ability to take it on, and yet I could see that at this point if the camp was to go ahead, there were few other options. As I considered my response, I was flicking through my Bible, and my eyes were drawn to this verse from 1 Chronicles, as if it leaped right off the page and spoke directly into my situation.

Here we see Solomon facing a similarly daunting task. His father, David, is nearing the end of his life, and Solomon is poised to take over from David as king. As if that wasn't enough of a challenge, Solomon has also been given the job to coordinate the building of the temple. As he considers this task, it is clear that his confidence is lacking. Even later, once he has taken over as king, the Bible records him praying about this. "Lord my God, you have now made your servant king in my father David's place. Yet I am just a youth with no experience in leadership" (1 Kings 3:7)

It is striking to look at how David encourages his son amid his lack of confidence in God and feelings of inadequacy. He doesn't just attempt to encourage Solomon that he can do it, that he has what it takes. He doesn't list the skills and attributes Solomon possesses which will equip him for what lies ahead. Instead, he is honest about Solomon's limitations and the magnitude of the task. "Then King David said to all the assembly, 'My son Solomon — God has chosen him alone — is young and

DAY 5

inexperienced. The task is great because the building will not be built for a human but for the Lord God'" (1 Chronicles 29:1).

He calls Solomon not to a confidence based on his own ability, but to a confidence in God because he was chosen for the task. He doesn't look to boost Solomon's self-esteem, but to encourage his confidence in the God who has called him.

- Not: "You can do this!" but "God is with you."
- Not: "You have all the skills you need!" but "God will see that the work is completed."
- Not: "Just work hard, and do your best!" but "Trust in God – He will not fail you or forsake you."

He calls him to confidence not in himself and his ability, but in God and His faithfulness.

Just as David's words encouraged Solomon to get on with the work of building the temple, they encouraged me, several years later, to get on with the work it had become clear God was calling me to — to step out in faith, putting my confidence in Him. It didn't make the task easy, and there were many challenges along the way, but, like Solomon, I saw God's faithfulness and experienced the truth that when God calls us, He enables us. Our confidence in Him is not misplaced.

Written By Lesley Crawford

DAY 5
QUESTIONS

What tasks are you being called to and how can you find your confidence in Him rather than your abilities alone?

Today I praise God for...

Today I am confessing...

Today I am praying for...

PRAYER

God, speak to my heart so that I can be confident in You when you call me to step out in faith for a task I don't feel equipped for. It isn't through my strength the job will be done but through Yours. Amen.

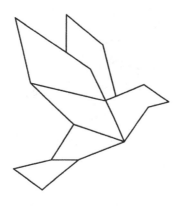

Cast your burden on the Lord,
and he will sustain you;
he will never allow the righteous to
be shaken.
Psalm 55:22

DAY 6

Is Worry a Sin?

"Therefore I tell you: Don't worry about your life, what you will eat or what you will drink; or about your body, what you will wear. Isn't life more than food and the body more than clothing?" Matthew 6:25

Worry is always sinful. Yes, I said it; worry is a sin. Worry is a sinful expression of fear, and a severe problem of the heart. It is a sin that many people struggle with on a day to day basis. It is a serious problem.

"Therefore I tell you: Don't worry about your life, what you will eat or what you will drink; or about your body, what you will wear. Isn't life more than food and the body more than clothing? Consider the birds of the sky: They don't sow or reap or gather into barns, yet your heavenly Father feeds them. Aren't you worth more than they? Can any of you add one moment to his life span by worrying? And why do you worry about clothes? Observe how the wildflowers of the field grow: They don't labor or spin thread. Yet I tell you that not even Solomon in all his splendor was adorned like one of these. If that's how God clothes the grass of the field, which is here today and thrown into the furnace tomorrow, won't he do much more for you—you of little

faith? So don't worry, saying, 'What will we eat?' or 'What will we drink?' or 'What will we wear?' For the Gentiles eagerly seek all these things, and your heavenly Father knows that you need them. But seek first the kingdom of God and his righteousness, and all these things will be provided for you. Therefore don't worry about tomorrow, because tomorrow will worry about itself. Each day has enough trouble of its own" (Matthew 6:25-34).

But what is worry? Worry and anxiety are ultimately different forms of fear rooted in a lack of understanding of Who God is and in a self-centered outlook on one's life and potential troubles. This then begs the question, "What is the Biblical solution to my worry?" Well, the Bible actually has quite a bit to say about worry, and one of the primary passages that deals with the issue of worry is here in Matthew 6:25-34. There are two major truths in this passage that will better equip you to deal with worry.

First, God is the sovereign provider. In verses 25-31, Jesus tells His disciples not to worry about their body, food, or clothes, but to instead consider how God provides for even the smallest and most insignificant of creatures. Essentially Jesus is making a greater than–less than comparison here. If God will feed the birds and clothe the flowers of the field, then why would He not provide for you who are made in His image and bought by the

DAY 6

blood of His Son? God is the sovereign provider Who is working all things out for His glory and the good of those who love Him. Yet, it is important to remember that this does not mean the Christian is exempt from suffering, persecution, sorrow, or loss. In fact, much of the New Testament promises that living for Christ will lead to suffering.

Even Paul says in Philippians that part of the Christian experience is to fellowship in Christ's sufferings (Philippians 3:10). You will face hardship and yet God still provides, though often in ways unexpected. For example, trials are an instrument for growth according to James 1:2-4. God often provides for you in ways that are least expected and sometimes even most undesired. Rest assured that God is sovereign and that He is working for your good and His glory. Even when it doesn't feel that way!

Second, Jesus equips us to battle worry by setting our eyes on the Kingdom and not ourselves. Worry is rooted in a constant desire for the well-being and benefit of self, and it expresses itself in concern for the future and desperate thoughts that plead, "What if?" Worry is often irrational and erratic self-centeredness that has the ability to consume the soul and cloud the mind. That is why Jesus says in verse 33 to seek God's kingdom first. He wants us, He wants you, to reroute the desire of your heart from

you to His kingdom. Paul echoes this very idea in Philippians 2 where he tells the Philippian believers to consider others more highly than themselves and to do nothing out of selfish ambition, but to look out for each other's interests (Philippians 2:3-4).

The antidote to your worry is to put the work of the kingdom before you and your needs and to put others first. To be selfless and to concern yourself not with your problems but with Christ's gospel. Know that God is your provider and seek first His Kingdom, not yours.

Written By Corbin Henderson

DAY 6
QUESTIONS

Understanding that worry is a sin and we're called to be sinless in all aspects of our life, where do you need confession and repentance from worry in your walk with the Lord?

Today I praise God for...

Today I am confessing...

Today I am praying for...

PRAYER

Dear Heavenly Father, show me today the areas of my life where I'm not putting You first. Convict me when I don't. Help me confess the sin of worry in my life and turn from that habit if it is present. Amen.

DAY 7

The Best Way to Cast out Fear

"Let love be without hypocrisy. Detest evil; cling to what is good." Romans 12:9

Have you ever heard the children's song *O Be Careful, Little Eyes*? The first verse urges us to be careful about what we see with our eyes, because our Father in heaven knows our true intentions. How can we be faithful with our eyes, loving God with everything we see, and cast out fear in our lives?

October is always a tough month for me, because I see so many images of evil, fear, and death. While others seem to enjoy tinkering with fear, I become a cornered wolverine when another Friday the 13th commercial pierces my peaceful evening. But fearful media doesn't return to its home in the underground come November 1, so I've had year-round practice turning my inner wolverine into a laid-back otter.

The Apostle Paul provides an answer in the Book of Romans. "Let love be without hypocrisy. Detest evil; cling to what is good" (Romans 12:9). The Greek word for *abhor* comes from a root meaning *separation*. So to *abhor* evil is more than hating how it makes you feel. It means taking action to separate yourself from evil, whether it's images, sounds, words, or actions.

I love Scripture because our God is so practical. Not only does He tell us what not to do, but He also tells us what we should do: Don't flirt with evil; instead, cling to what is good. In Philippians 4:8, we get a wonderful list of things to cling to. "Finally brothers and sisters, whatever is true, whatever is honorable, whatever is just, whatever is pure, whatever is lovely, whatever is commendable — if there is any moral excellence and if there is anything praiseworthy — dwell on these things."

Philippians 4:8 is a beautiful litmus test. Are your little eyes viewing truth, nobility, purity, love, goodness, or virtue? If not, consider turning the channel, closing the browser, looking away, walking away, whatever it takes to separate yourself, and cast out fear from your life.

God is love, and there is no fear in love. So if we want to be more like God, and love without hypocrisy, then we should seek truth, choose virtue, and cling to the praiseworthy media we discover, knowing that your Father is looking down in love.

Written By Valerie Riese

DAY 7
QUESTIONS

How can I be more proactive about filtering the things I consume that add to my fear and anxiety?

Today I praise God for...

Today I am confessing...

Today I am praying for...

PRAYER

Father, thank You for Your Word, full of goodness and truth. Thank You for giving us clear, practical instructions to separate ourselves from fear, to grow in love, and to become more like You. Please forgive me for the times I've chosen anything that wasn't praiseworthy in Your eyes, and I ask for better

discernment in the future. Most of all, Father, thank You for giving Your only Son, Jesus, to save me from the eternity of evil I deserve. Amen.

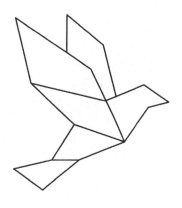

The chains of love are stronger than

the chains of fear.

- William Gurnall

DAY 8

How Do I Overcome My Unbelief?

"Jesus said to him, 'If you can'? Everything is possible for the one who believes.' Immediately the father of the boy cried out, 'I do believe; help my unbelief!'" Mark 9:23-24

I imagine he was mentally and emotionally exhausted. For years he searched unsuccessfully for the healing his son needed. He tried everything within his own power, but his son's suffering continued. Desperate for something—anything—to work, he turned to Jesus. We find the account of this man's story in the books of Matthew, Mark, and Luke. At a very young age, an evil spirit possessed the boy. We aren't given the details around the years nor the search for healing. But the story starts with the man and his son in the middle of an arguing crowd. He and his son set off to find this Jesus who many were talking about. When they arrived, Jesus was not there. However, some of His disciples were there, and it was said that they, too, had the power to heal. So, he asked them to cast out the evil spirit possessing his son. The disciples attempted to do so but failed.

Not long after, Jesus appeared. Frustrated, "He replied to them, 'You unbelieving generation, how long will I be with you? How long must I put up with you? Bring him to me'" (Mark 9:19).

The father explained the details of his son's affliction then pleaded with Jesus, "And many times it has thrown him into fire or water to destroy him. But if you can do anything, have compassion on us and help us" (Mark 9:22).

There's a line in the text that tells us a great deal about the man and his unbelief. He said, "if you can." He wasn't convinced of Jesus' power to do all things—including healing his son.

This man's story of unbelief may resonate with you right now. For some it's been a difficult year. Some faced trials they never saw coming or would have believed possible. We all face trials of many kinds—trials that don't line up with our vision of a just God. Trials that bring us to our knees in pain.

Maybe you once wrestled with or are right now wrestling with unbelief after facing painful circumstances and you need help with lingering doubts. Or maybe it is the opposite. You've always wrestled with unbelief, but now your pain is giving you cause to long for more. More hope. More faith. More Jesus.

How do I overcome my unbelief?

1. In order to overcome unbelief, we must be willing to surrender it all. We must surrender the belief that we can do it all on our own. Whether it is our own wisdom, ability, or finances, they all come to an end. We and our resources are finite.

DAY 8

2. In order to overcome unbelief, we must have a burning desire to replace our worldly desires with the things of God. Faith is His gift to us. We simply can't hold tightly to the things of the world and experience the fullness of faith at the same time.

3. In order to overcome unbelief, we must ask God for help.

So what happened to the father in our story? Jesus basically answered the boy's father with the question, "What do you mean, if I can? Anything is possible if a person believes." (See verse 23). At that moment the boy's father took those last two steps. By bringing his son to Jesus, he demonstrated the realization that he was limited in his own power. But in the moments as he looked into the eyes of Jesus and heard Him speak the Truth, he knew his belief must come with surrender. Only God could give him the gift of true belief – true faith. He cried out to Jesus, telling Him he believed, but that he needed help with the remaining unbelief—a humble surrender from a man who finally understood.

Belief doesn't mean God will always answer our prayers the way we want. It means we believe that He can. This story tells us God hears our cries no matter the size of our belief. He wants us to come to Him even when our faith is small and our unbelief big

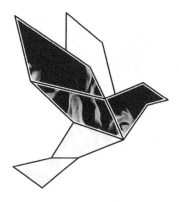

because He is in the business of transformation. He uses those moments when we fall at His feet in surrender to confirm our faith and remind us how great His love and mercy for us is. None of us are perfect believers, but as we surrender and ask God for help, we make progress toward experiencing the fullness of a faith that knows anything is possible with Christ.

Written By Lori Schumaker

DAY 8
QUESTIONS

Name the area in your life that carries the most fear and anxiety and write practical steps you can take to give that to God.

Today I praise God for...

Today I am confessing...

Today I am praying for...

PRAYER

Father, I know my faith is not perfect, but I long for more. Lord, help me overcome my unbelief. Give me eyes to see and a spirit of willingness to lay down my pride. I know my strength and my resources are limited. They are finite. But You, Father, are infinite in Your wisdom, love, mercy, grace, and power. You start where I end. In Jesus' name, I pray, Amen.

DAY 9

Do Not Fear

"For God has not given us a spirit of fear, but one of power, love, and sound judgment" 2 Timothy 1:7

These days, it seems like fear is everywhere. Even so, God's Word is filled with Scripture telling us "do not fear." But how are we supposed to achieve such a tall order? Who are we, against the wickedness that permeates this world? Royalty, that's who.

We are sons and daughters of the Most High God. We are betrothed to the King of kings and Lord of lords and are His co-heirs. We are also a royal priesthood. And as royalty, we have been given authority by the Maker and Master of the universe. How much authority? Jesus Himself tells us in Luke 10:19, "Look, I have given you the authority to trample on snakes and scorpions and over all the power of the enemy; nothing at all will harm you."

Don't miss this. That's a lot of authority! He even admitted in the next verse that, although we are not to be doing fist bumps and victory dances over the fact that the demons are subject to us in His name, nevertheless, they are subject to us in His name.

Do any of the political leaders in the highest offices, or the world's most powerful kings, have this kind of authority? Not

if they don't belong to Jesus. And if any do belong to Jesus, they have this authority only because He gave it to them as royal children of God.

We tend to forget who we are in Christ – or worse, have never been taught in the first place. We also tend to forget or have yet to be taught that there's a colossal, unseen war going on in the spiritual realm, twenty-four seven. The servant of the great prophet Elisha experienced this truth firsthand.

The king of Syria made the mistake of going to war with the king of Israel, but each time he outlined his plans to his servants, including where he intended to place his camp, Elisha would go and warn the king of Israel, who would then avoid the king of Syria. After his plans were foiled several times, the Syrian king called his servants together and declared that one of them must be a traitor. But one of them explained that the prophet Elisha was to blame, pointing out that, "…'No one, my lord the king. Elisha, the prophet in Israel, tells the king of Israel even the words you speak in your bedroom'" (2 Kings 6:12).

Thinking to pluck out this thorn in his side, the Syrian king had Elisha tracked down to the city of Dothan. He then proceeded to send a great army, including plenty of horses and chariots, to surround the city by night.

When Elisha's servant got up the next morning and went out,

DAY 9

he was greeted by a terrifying sight – the Syrian army had them surrounded! Horrified, the servant cried out to Elisha, "What shall we do?" Cool as a cucumber, Elisha told him to fear not, because those who were with them were more numerous than those who were against them. To make his point, the prophet then asked God to open the man's eyes so he could see into the spiritual world. God did so, and the servant saw that the mountain was full of horses and not just ordinary chariots, but chariots of fire.

"But what about me?" you may be thinking. I can't see into the spirit realm. I can't see the warrior angels who serve God fighting the evil ones. More than likely, the spiritual realm will remain invisible, but like the wind, sound waves, and so many other things, just because we don't see them doesn't mean they're not there. And just because we don't see the cosmic battles going on, doesn't mean we can't fight, too. And fight we must.

Yes, Jesus is the Lord of the Heavenly armies, and He fights on our behalf. But He also gave us a set of armor, along with a shield and sword, for a reason. In Ephesians 6:11-17, Paul reminds us who we are fighting against and to make sure we're dressed for battle and armed. We are to do our part and not sit passively on the fence, wringing our hands in fear.

But what about our lives in the here and now? As we look

around, we may be dismayed, as it seems the world is going to hell in a hand basket.

The apostle John tells us, "Do not love the world or the things in the world." See 1 John 2:15-17. Does this mean that wanting a happy life and nice things is bad? No, wanting these things is not bad in and of itself.

But the world and, to some extent, the things we desire – houses, vacations, jobs, security, relationships, etc. are like red herrings thrown out by Satan. While there may be nothing wrong with wanting these things, we must remember, they are all passing away. It's when we make these things into idols that we get into trouble. The devil knows this, and in order to get us to take our eyes off the eternal prize, that's what he goads us to do, then he packages up the worldly desires into pretty boxes and throws them out like red herrings to distract us. Those distractions are two-fold: not only do we get distracted from focusing on the things of God and eternity, but we also get distracted from seeing Satan's wicked chess game, with humanity as his unsuspecting pawns. And we fear. Sometimes to the point of being paralyzed by all the what-ifs.

Look up. Your redemption draws near.

Written By Lynn Churchill

DAY 9
QUESTIONS

Like Elisha, where have you seen spiritual warfare and how can you be a soldier in God's army to help fight those battles?

_____

_____

_____

_____

Today I praise God for...

_____

_____

_____

Today I am confessing...

_____

_____

_____

Today I am praying for...

_____

_____

_____

PRAYER

God of angel armies, don't let me buy into the devil's lies. Help me not to fear. This world is passing away. Help me keep my eyes on You knowing there is a better world to be had, far better than my wildest imaginations. Amen.

DAY 10

Do Not Fear For I Am with You

"Do not fear, for I am with you; do not be afraid, for I am your God. I will strengthen you; I will help you; I will hold on to you with my righteous right hand" Isaiah 41:10

Last spring, I underwent a serious but fairly routine surgery for a uterine tumor. As I laid in the recovery room, all my vital signs were stable. My husband visited and kissed me goodbye to go home and check on our children. I was coming out of anesthesia and everything seemed to have gone well. I was so relieved and was feeling at peace over the whole surgery.

Earlier, I had prayed for God's healing and protection, wisdom and skill for the doctors, and I remember thinking to myself, "It's all over, now I can begin to recover and heal." Breathing a sigh of relief, I closed my eyes. I heard one of the nurses come in to take my blood pressure and other vital signs and then heard her quickly rush out of the room. Within the next few minutes, my surgeon and several nurses surrounded me. The questions came, "Do you feel ok?" "Do you understand what we are saying?" "Does anything hurt?" I was completely coherent and told them I felt fine.

I could see other doctors rushing in: a cardiologist, an internal

medicine doctor, another surgeon, and numerous other nurses and hospital staff. I heard one of them say, "Her blood pressure has dropped to 50/40 and we cannot find any reason for it. We need to stabilize her quickly." I didn't realize the seriousness of the situation until I saw a doctor enter the room with the "crash cart" and I heard a nurse whisper, "The chief hospital physician is here." My heart began to beat harder in my chest and fear set in. Anxiety and a sense of dread overtook me. I remember thinking, "Oh my goodness, I am dying!"

Closing my eyes, I prayed very simply, "Jesus, I trust You. Give me courage and peace, take away my fear. I trust You with my life." You see, friends, as I heard the panic around me, I quickly realized the direness of the situation. Medical tests were run, CT scans and other imaging analyzed, and I was growing tired. I was told I was very pale and my breathing labored. It would have been easy to try and rely on my own courage and strength, especially in this situation. But I knew this was beyond my own control. Beyond my own courage. My life was in God's hands. I released my fear to Him. I did the only thing I knew how to do…pray.

Scripture tells us repeatedly that God hears our prayers and that He is always with us. He numbers our days and is in complete control of our lives. I could feel His presence in my

DAY 10

hospital room, and I knew at that moment I was going to be ok. With my prayers came complete peace. Even as I was rushed into emergency surgery for internal bleeding, I knew God was in control.

As I prayed for courage and strength, God showed up in great ways. He took my fear and anxious thoughts and replaced them with His peace. A peace that transcends all understanding. This peace remained as I was transferred into the ICU where I stayed for several days recovering. This peace was my courage as I underwent three days of blood and platelet transfusions, and it remained as I received a cancer diagnosis shortly thereafter.

We see stories in the Bible in which God gave great courage to those who placed their trust in Him. Daniel 6 tells the story of Daniel refusing to stop honoring God in prayer and how he was thrown into the den of lions to be eaten alive. But God gave Daniel courage and strength, staying by his side, and in the end, we saw Daniel's life spared. When we release our fear to God, He, in turn, gives us courage and peace for every situation. God wants to show up in big ways in our lives. As we pray in faith for courage and strength, we can then watch expectantly for Him to do miraculous things. Have you released your fears to God? Today is a perfect day to start living in His courage and peace!

Written By Pamela Keener

DAY 10
QUESTIONS

What situation in your life do you need to release to God, allowing him to provide a peace that passes understanding?

Today I praise God for...

Today I am confessing...

Today I am praying for...

PRAYER

Jesus, I trust You. Give me courage and peace, take away my fear. I trust You with my life. Amen.

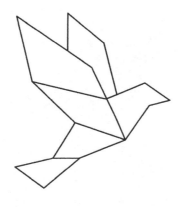

Faith, which is trust, and fear are opposite poles. If a man has the one, he can scarcely have the other in vigorous operation. He that has his trust set upon God does not need to dread anything except the weakening or the paralyzing of that trust.

- Alexander MacLaren

DAY 11

Circle of Life

"I call heaven and earth as witnesses against you today that I have set before you life and death, blessing and curse. Choose life so that you and your descendants may live, love the Lord your God, obey him, and remain faithful to him. For he is your life, and he will prolong your days as you live in the land the Lord swore to give to your ancestors Abraham, Isaac, and Jacob" Deuteronomy 30:19-20

God's Kingdom rests on the three elements of freedom, choice, and love. The interaction of these elements, which are intertwined and interdependent, is what I call the "circle of life." Freedom and choice are requirements for love to exist. Without freedom, we have no ability to choose. Without the ability to choose, we cannot love. The very character and definition of love requires that it be freely given as a choice and that it cannot be mandated or forced. In other words, God's own nature cannot be extricated from this circle of life.

Scripture emphasizes the importance of our freedom, telling us, "Now the Lord is the Spirit, and where the Spirit of the Lord is, there is freedom" (II Corinthians 3:17); "For freedom, Christ set us free. Stand firm, then, and don't submit again to a yoke of slavery"

(Galatians 5:1); and, "For you were called to be free, brothers and sisters; only don't use this freedom as an opportunity for the flesh, but serve one another through love" (Galatians 5:13).

Scripture also establishes the importance of our choices See Deuteronomy 30:19-20.

Finally, Jesus made clear that everything hinges on love when He taught, "Love the Lord your God with all your heart, with all your soul, with all your strength, and with all your mind, and your neighbor as yourself" (Luke 10:27).

Every action and response of God comes from His heart of love for you. Scripture tells us God is love (I John 4:8), and being Himself love, He could do nothing else but act in love. So, if something is not loving, it is not coming from God. This concept is so powerful and so deeply meaningful to how we view God, and thus how we relate to God, it deserves serious contemplation. If we do not believe this truth, we are vulnerable to all kinds of deceptions that ascribe to God things that are actually the result of the actions of the enemy. Not seeing God through the lens of freedom, choice, and love causes us to misinterpret Scripture, to falsely blame God for bad things that happen to us, and ultimately to distance ourselves from God or even reject God.

Satan offers us counterfeits for the "circle of life." Instead of freedom, he offers control. He encourages us to try to "control,"

DAY 11

or he deceives us into giving into the "control" of external forces. Because control feels more stable and secure to us, we are easily persuaded to abdicate our freedom in exchange for that illusion.

Instead of choice, Satan presents fear and worry. We are convinced by listening to fear and following where it leads or worrying about what is to come. We will keep ourselves from getting hurt, but Jesus tells us the opposite: "Can any of you add one moment to his life span by worrying?" (Luke 12:25).

Instead of love, Satan offers shame and condemnation. He sets us up to judge ourselves and others, preventing love from flowing from our hearts or receiving love from God, and convinces us we deserve condemnation. Paul counters Satan's argument by saying, "Therefore, there is now no condemnation for those in Christ Jesus, because the law of the Spirit of life in Christ Jesus has set you free from the law of sin and death" (Romans 8:1-2).

Like God's "circle of life," Satan's counterfeits are interdependent and interconnected. When I try to control, such as closing off my heart to protect myself or hiding behind a false smile, I realize I have no control and I feel fear, which leads to shame because I believe I "should" be more capable. Out of my shame, I try harder to control, creating a self-reinforcing circle. Through this "circle of death," Satan attempts to restrict our

freedom to choose, because he knows limiting choice means limiting love, both in the giving and in the receiving of love. Shame also limits love, because we soon believe we do not deserve to be loved and reject the gift of God's love freely offered to us. Satan will tell us repeatedly we should, we have to, we can't, and we must, each of which limits our choices. Ultimately, he will use this "circle of death" as proof that we are worthless and unloved.

When we step out of the "circle of life," we enter Satan's "circle of death" and begin a spiral into our own destruction. Jesus, however, always offers us a pathway into the "circle of life" through His truth.

If you find yourself believing fear or shame or feeling in control or out of control, powerless, or trapped, go over the verses listed above to fight against the enemy's lies, then turn to Jesus and ask Him what truth replaces these lies. When reduced to its foundations, every truth has its origins in the love of Christ for us. He loved us enough to make us partners and co-heirs with Him and to give us the freedom to choose Him, so we can truly love Him and receive His love.

Written By Dr. Donna E. Lane

DAY 11
QUESTIONS

In what area of your life do you need to let freedom, choice, or love reign more? How is Satan using one of those to limit your ability to love others?

Today I praise God for...

Today I am confessing...

Today I am praying for...

PRAYER

Loving God, help me to stay in Your Word so that I will know the difference between Satan's lies and Your truth. In Jesus' name, Amen.

DAY 12

Faith through Fear

"Though the fig tree does not bud and there is no fruit on the vines, though the olive crop fails and the fields produce no food, though the flocks disappear from the pen and there are no herds in the stalls, yet I will celebrate in the Lord; I will rejoice in the God of my salvation!" Habakkuk 3:17-18

What is your worst fear? I remember years ago, sitting in a Bible study full of young moms like myself when our leader asked us each to think about what our worst fear might be. I could see the other women thinking. With all of our minds occupied with naps and diapers and play dates, fear wasn't something most of us spent time contemplating on a regular basis. But not me. I knew what my greatest fear was because I thought about it every day. As we went around the room that morning, most of my friends' fears were pretty predictable — losing a child or losing their husband, etc. Those fears made me feel jealous because they were remote. Yes, those things happen every day, and I fear those things too, but they weren't likely to happen.

My fear, on the other hand, was a 50/50 opportunity. My father inherited a genetic disease that caused a gradual loss of

brain function, diminishing his physical and mental ability over eight years. As I sat in the Bible study that morning he was in the end stages of his disease. A year later he would be gone, shortly after his 59th birthday. My biggest fear that morning was that I was the next in line to receive a painful genetic inheritance that stretches back several generations.

It has been several years since my father moved into his home in heaven, and I still don't know if this is in my future. But the fear lingers. I am afraid of the emotional pain I may experience as I gradually lose the ability to think and act for myself, and I grieve for my husband and children who would need to care for me and encounter the same fear I walk with now.

Though I spent most of the first two years of grieving feeling angry, God led me to recovery and to a shift in how I lived with this fear. As I grow closer to the age my father was when he began losing his memory, I have a distinct advantage. I get the opportunity to look this fear in the face and to learn to live with it, grow with it, and make friends with it. The fear isn't going away. But living with a fear like this has fine-tuned my perspective on how being a child of God should shape my life and how I spend it. Am I walking in faith, or am I allowing my fears to become my motivators? Does what I'm doing on this day, or this hour, or this minute, reflect my role as a witness for Christ? Do my children

DAY 12

see Jesus in me? Does my life help them see the value of walking with God, even through the darkest valley?

The prophet Habakkuk's prophecies are unique in that he did not address them to the people of Israel and Judah, but to God on their behalf. In the process of creating this letter to God, Habakkuk learns of the coming Babylonian captivity, and he and God engage in a poetic call and response as God explains His anger at the people's unfaithfulness to Him. Habakkuk laments its result in prayer. And then, just a few verses prior to the close of his book, Habakkuk makes a remarkable profession of faith. "Though the fig tree does not bud and there is no fruit on the vines, though the olive crop fails and the fields produce no food, though the flocks disappear from the pen and there are no herds in the stalls, yet I will celebrate in the Lord; I will rejoice in the God of my salvation!" (Habakkuk 3:17-18).

Even after learning God is angry with Habakkuk's people, and the result of that anger will be the complete destruction of their home and exile of its inhabitants, Habakkuk makes the choice to celebrate and rejoice. His words here are a commitment to faith in God's love for His people, even as they reap the results of their sin. Even in the face of exile and death.

When we look at God's Word, His love story for His children, Habakkuk's reaction makes sense, but when we look at the world

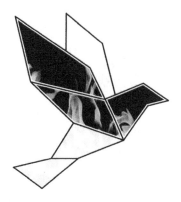

around us, full of crime, dishonesty, pain, and all other forms of destruction that come from our sinfulness, Habakkuk's faith seems like nonsense. In our faith walks, we are faced with the dichotomy of God's love for mankind and the sinfulness of the world, and sometimes that frustrates me, especially when I see it in myself.

I want to reflect God's love for my children, but I get angry and yell at them instead. I want to speak loving truth to a friend living in sin, but I chicken out. Praise God that His love for us isn't diminished by my weakness, but that instead my weakness, even my fears, allow His love to be perfected (2 Cor. 12:9). My faith walk through fear is now made up of many different pieces. I love my husband, my kids, my friends, and I try to love people in general. I write about my faith, and I encourage students who need help with their own writing. I'm learning not to be afraid to let the dishes sit in the sink while I meditate, or read, or just rest. I volunteered to sing for my church's worship team, and I might even join a rock band. It's not skydiving, but it's daring.

You don't need to be facing death or disease to live like you're dying. Don't let fear prevent you from finding out what God is calling you to and doing it.

Written By Melanie Makovsky

DAY 12
QUESTIONS

If you found out you had a terminal illness tomorrow, what would change about your life and faith walk? Does that need to happen for you to start living without fear?

Today I praise God for...

Today I am confessing...

Today I am praying for...

PRAYER

Lord, I'm choosing today to live like I'm dying because I am, even if I don't know when or how just yet. More importantly, I'm choosing to remember that this world is not my home and that both little discomforts and huge trials can simply remind me that I'm not there yet. Amen.

DAY 13

To Fear God

"Whoever lives with integrity fears the Lord, but the one who is devious in his ways despises him" Proverbs 14:2

One of the ways a person can know they are right before God is whether or not they fear Him. Fear is one of the things that characterized people before Calvary. The law of God taught His children to fear Him. It was very clear that if man did not obey God, there was an eternal price to pay. God's children understood that you don't mess with God. God is holy and will not condone or tolerate sinful living by His children.

At Calvary, Jesus took upon Himself the wrath of God. He did for us what the law could not do; He provided a way for us to know God on a personal level. We now live in grace and therefore the edge of fear has gone away. But, is that a good thing? I personally believe we should still have a sense of fear for God. If there were a greater fear of God, there would be greater respect for Him shown. There would be more careful living; sin would matter more to us than it does today. We have lost the sense of need to strive to be holy since Jesus is our holiness. We become spiritually lazy and rest solely on the finished work of Christ at Calvary on our behalf.

Now, don't get me wrong. We cannot make ourselves holy by what we do. We cannot save ourselves by what we do. We cannot be accepted by God as His own without embracing the finished work of Christ on Calvary. We cannot do for ourselves what Christ has done for us. We are saved by faith in Christ alone; it is a gift of God. We just cannot use our new relationship with God as an excuse for not fearing Him.

Those who try to get to God any other way than through Christ despise God. All other attempts to reach God are futile and cause man to express his frustrations over the emptiness and hopelessness of his life. Man tries to look good in his own eyes; he tries to do his best and do things his way. He hates God and His ways because it leaves man falling short. It is a slap in man's face to be told he is not good enough, that he will not enter into heaven without Christ. Man wants to be in control and when he is told he cannot be in control and be right with God, it causes him to rebel and despise those who declare Jesus to be the way, truth, and life.

Choose the right path today. Fear God and turn away from evil and you will make it to heaven when you die.

Written By Jim Hughes

DAY 13
QUESTIONS

Knowing that a reverent fear of God is good, in what areas of your life should you re-evaluate your piety to God?

Today I praise God for...

Today I am confessing...

Today I am praying for...

PRAYER

God, I want to have a healthy fear of You as the saints of old did. I want to respect You and love You and know that only You are the Way, the Truth, and the Life. In Your holy name, Amen.

DAY 14

Healthy Fear

"For learning wisdom and discipline; for understanding insightful sayings" Proverbs 1:2

When my son was a toddler, just learning to stand up on his own, all he wanted to do was run. He didn't want to walk. He ran. He had no fear. He didn't even have the smart kind of fear. This was scariest when we were at the beach. We'd be setting up our umbrella and picnic blankets, and he'd sprint for the water having no concept of swimming or drowning. He needed to learn a little bit about healthy fear.

One has to learn how to fear God. In the Old Testament, the fear of God was a guiding principle for every aspect of life for as long as one lived on the earth.

"For learning wisdom and discipline; for understanding insightful sayings" (Proverbs 1:2).

This verse and the verses that follow give the purpose and payoff of Proverbs. It's an intensely practical book, applicable to every aspect of your life. It's intellectual. It engages and exercises your brain. It's moral. Justice, equity, and righteousness are constant themes because they make sense. There was as much of an appetite for this in the ancient world as there is now. They

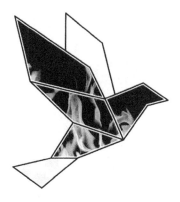

flow from the heart of God into and through His people.

Proverbs features three conspicuous characters throughout its pages: the simple, the fool, and the wise. The simple man doesn't commit, he's easily misled, and doesn't apply himself to discipline. This person needs to get Proverbs up and running in his life.

The fool is opposed to God's covenant, resists forgiveness, is a dangerous influence, and causes grief to his parents. The scary thing about the fool is that he moves freely among God's people. Believe it or not, he is not beyond hope.

The wise person embraces the principles learned in this book. He makes good progress and is an example worth following. God desires that you be a wise person. That's why He made sure this book found its way into your hands.

Proverbs begs to be probed, searched, and questioned closely. Proper relation to God involves trying hard to understand His truth and applying what you've learned. This book is not written for learning how to live life so that someday you'll go to heaven when you die. It is written to teach you how to live in the fear of God, in the here and now, until you are present with Him in His kingdom.

Now, go equip others to do the same.

Written By Bryon Mondok

DAY 14
QUESTIONS

How can you take the Proverbs and other scripture and apply them to your life to become wise and develop healthy fear?

Today I praise God for...

Today I am confessing...

Today I am praying for...

PRAYER

Heavenly Father, You tell us to hide Your Word in our hearts. Help me to be like the wise man in Proverbs who not only reads the Word but takes it to heart and teaches others Your truths. Amen.

DAY 15

Seek God's Kingdom

"But seek first the kingdom of God and His righteousness, and all these things will be provided for you." Matthew 6:33

I'm a worrier. I've spent much of my life battling anxiety and fear that has left me paralyzed, or at the very least, nauseous and uninterested in food. I've found myself crying out more often and more anxiously. "God, I need You to come through. I need You to provide because I really don't know how I'm going to get through the month." In response, God has brought me back to this passage in Matthew I've read more times than I can count. It's a section from Jesus' Sermon on the Mount where He addresses the issue of worry. He says simply, "Do not worry" because our heavenly Father knows what we need. To help emphasize His point, Jesus uses the birds and the lilies as examples of God's care for His creation. The birds don't store up food, yet they are provided for. The lilies of the field don't toil or spin their own clothes, yet they are beautifully clothed. For years, in the midst of so much anxiety, this passage, and God's care for the birds, has given me comfort.

In this season, though, God has drawn my focus away from the birds to a verse tucked in near the end. "But seek first the

kingdom of God and his righteousness, and all these things will be provided for you" (Matthew 6:33). What does it mean to seek God's kingdom first? Even when the Bible isn't open in front of me, that verse has been playing on repeat in my mind. I memorized it years ago in Sunday school, but I'm wondering what it means for me right now? Jesus spends a whole lot of time addressing worry, but I think the beginning of this passage is a set up for Him to talk about the kingdom.

The cure to anxiety isn't found in not worrying. I've tried not worrying, and it only generates more worry. No, the cure to anxiety is found when we look up from our anxiety and seek God's kingdom first. It's here where you're probably circling back to the same question I've been asking: What does it mean to seek God's kingdom? Here are a few things I've come to understand about what it means to seek God's kingdom in the midst of anxiety:

Seeking God's kingdom means trusting He will take care of your needs, despite how things look. We start here because Jesus starts here. When He is teaching the crowd about how to combat anxiety, He acknowledges the people's needs and His Father's ability to provide for those needs. The birds and flowers are taken care of, so we can trust that God will take care of us, His children, too. We don't need to strive or rush or wring our hands together,

DAY 15

wondering how we're going to make this work. We simply need to trust that He will come through because He said He would. We will have enough. We will have what we need.

Seeking God's kingdom means worshiping Him in the middle places. Anxiety stems out of concern for the future, for those places we've yet to reach. It's a form of control that says we have to have all the answers in order to feel safe. Knowing what lies ahead is a false sense of security, though. True security lies in the middle place, before we see God come through, before we see the provision. In that place, as shaky as it might feel, we can worship God right where we are because the truth of who He is never changes. Worshiping before we see the answer is challenging and downright hard, but if we approach God believing His promises and acknowledging no matter what, He is God and we want to see His kingdom come to earth, we can worship. Even in imperfect faith, we can worship.

Seeking God's kingdom means noticing the work God is doing in and around you and partnering with Him. Want a quick cure for anxiety? Turn your attention outward. Stop focusing on your needs and fears that God won't provide—Jesus already assured us He will, so you can take your eyes off that need. Instead, look up and look around. Notice where God is at work in your family, your community, and your heart. Ask Him how you

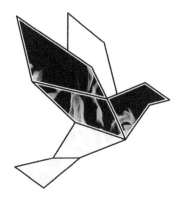

can partner with Him in that work. Ask Him how you can be an agent of helping those around you experience God's kingdom. To seek God's kingdom first we need to cultivate a heart that says we not only want to experience God in our own lives, but we want our world to experience Him too.

It's so easy to let anxiety rule in our hearts and get all twisted up with so many concerns about how our needs are going to be met. Jesus tells us not to worry, and for good reason. The Father knows our needs and has promised to take care of us. Our job is to lay all our anxiety and worry and fear at the Father's feet and seek His kingdom, trusting that He will take care of us just like He promised.

Written By Jazmin Frank

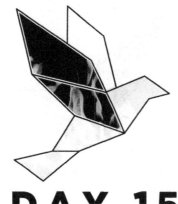

DAY 15
QUESTIONS

Where can you find opportunities to serve God in your family or community that will help take the attention off your anxiety and put your feet to work serving the Kingdom.

Today I praise God for...

Today I am confessing...

Today I am praying for...

PRAYER

Lord, help me to simply lay all my burdens at Your feet. Help me to seek Your kingdom daily. Help me to worship you in the here and now, and put aside the anxiety I have over the unknown future I have no control over. Help me to notice the work You're doing all around me. Amen.

DAY 16

Lifting the Weight
of an Anxious Heart

"A person's anxiety will weigh him down, but an encouraging word makes him joyful." Proverbs 12:25 GW

It's an epidemic. Opioid addiction has become a national epidemic in America. But it's not only opioid-based medications that are a problem. A myriad of disorders ranging from depression to behavioral problems has brought a plague of prescription drugs on our nation. Pain isn't always physical. When a person has an anxious heart, it's painful—a heavy, penetrating pain. America may be a rich and powerful nation, but we're weighed down with worry and can't seem to get out from under this burden without a prescription.

But there is another way to deal with an anxious heart. It is surprising and simple. It doesn't require a doctor's appointment, a prescription, or any specialized training. Anxiety may weigh a person down, but an encouraging word makes him joyful. It may seem too simplistic. Indeed, some psychological disorders may still require treatment and medications, but genuine and meaningful encouragement is still helpful, even in severe cases. I've seen this firsthand.

Words are powerful. They can tear down or build someone up. They're rarely neutral. What we hear plays back in our minds over and over, like a never-ending recording. It's called self-talk. Destructive words go deep. They penetrate our hearts and embed themselves in our minds. Careless words stab like a sword (Proverbs 12:18). It doesn't matter who utters these piercing words. When spoken by those we're closest to — parents, a spouse, siblings, children, significant others, friends, people at work or school — their wounding words go deep.

So, how can we counter this internal wound? How can you and I deal with worries and wounding words? We all need to hear encouraging words of truth often and from people we trust. People who are trustworthy. Those whom we know genuinely care about us. Likewise, we need to speak encouraging words and be genuine and trustworthy to others.

Here is the counter to the words that "stab like a sword": "Careless words stab like a sword, but the words of wise people bring healing." (Proverbs 12:18 GW). Notice it says, "words." Not casual or trite statements like — "Oh, they didn't really mean that" or, "Just ignore what they say." We need to hear genuine and encouraging words. These words need to come from people wise enough to know what we need and what is appropriate. They also need to be words of truth. "The word of truth lasts

DAY 16

forever, but lies last only a moment." (Proverbs 12:19 GW).

If you have an anxious heart and you're weighed down with many words, you need to be around people you trust. People who can encourage you with the truth. Where? Church is a good place to start, but I know too that some people in churches may speak wounding words. We need to seek a community of believers who are accepting and loving in a biblical but nonjudgmental way. It could be a church or a small group connected to a church or ministry. There are no quick fixes with prescriptive words and phrases. Bible quotes are nice but too often spoken in trite ways (see James 2:15-16). A continuous flow of encouraging truth is the only way healing and restoration go deep enough in our hearts and minds. This will lighten the load of worries and wounds we encounter.

When your heart is anxious and weighed down with many worries, you need to be around people you trust. Ask God to help you see encouraging words in His written Word, the Bible. If you don't have encouraging people around you, ask the Lord to help you find people you can trust and who are encouraging and ask for His help to be the same way for them.

Written By Trip Kimball

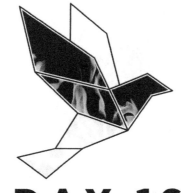

DAY 16
QUESTIONS

Do you have people in your life that speak encouraging words to you? If not, where can you go to find them? Who can you speak encouraging words to today?

_____

_____

_____

Today I praise God for...

_____

_____

Today I am confessing...

_____

_____

Today I am praying for...

_____

_____

_____

PRAYER

God, when I need an encouraging word, I pray You provide that for me, whether from another person or from Your Word. If someone else needs encouragement, send me. Amen.

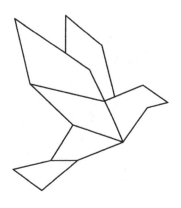

For God has not given us a spirit of fear, but one of power, love, and sound judgment.

2 Timothy 1:7

DAY 17

Distracted by Worry and Wants

"Don't strive for what you should eat and what you should drink, and don't be anxious. For the Gentile world eagerly seeks all these things, and your Father knows that you need them. But seek his kingdom, and these things will be provided for you" Luke 12:29-31

Years ago, I flew to Chicago with my husband to visit his father. We landed just in time for lunch, but that wasn't on the agenda...at least according to my father-in-law. He was just so excited to show us around Chicago—his hometown—that he didn't want to slow down for a silly lunch stop. He took us on an all-points tour of the (then) Sears Tower, Lake Michigan, Moody Bible Institute, Wrigley Field, his old stomping grounds, as well as the family bike shop off Diversey Avenue, just to name a few hotspots. Unfortunately, my father-in-law had no idea how little I was paying attention to his tour of Chicagoland. My stomach had taken over my brain and all I was "worrying" about was getting something to eat, and eating soon! Finally, by 4 p.m., he decided it was time for us to go get and experience a "Chicago-style" hot dog. It was then, and then only, that I was able to focus on where I was and whom we came to visit.

This story illustrates the tension we all often feel in life to fixate on temporal things. Typically, the "things" we worry about are not eating or drinking on any given day. But we can easily become distracted by some personal desire in our lives—letting it pull us away from the most important focus for life. I don't know about you, but I can be trucking along and doing just fine in my faith walk. In those moments, I'm able to stay focused on God, His kingdom, and kingdom purposes, all because my life is going well and my stomach is well fed. But the moment my earthly appetites emerge—whatever they might be—I'm tempted to turn away from an undivided focus on God and worry about my next earthly "fix."

Yet, you and I will never be ultimately satisfied by what this world provides. For me, that Chicago hot dog didn't go very far. I was hungry for another meal just a few short hours later. And it's the same way with any appetite that we focus on or worry about in life.

The only true and lasting satisfaction is found in a complete and undivided focus on God. Does that mean we should ignore our hunger pangs? That's not the point of Jesus' words here! But it does mean that our hunger for "stuff" should never become so all-consuming that we end up turning our attention away from God. Best of all, Jesus offers an amazing promise to us in verse

DAY 17

31. When we keep our focus completely on Him day in and day out—"these things will be provided for you."

Some could easily interpret this to mean God will give us everything we want from this life on earth. However, this is really about God giving us everything we want and need in our eternal life in His kingdom. That reward and blessing, my friends, is way more glorious and satisfying than anything this earth can provide—including a Chicago-style hot dog! Oh yeah! Way, way better than that!

Written By Beth Steffaniak

DAY 17
QUESTIONS

What earthly appetite has captured your attention and pulled you away from an undivided focus on God? What is one thing you can do today to release your grip from that desire?

Today I praise God for...

Today I am confessing...

Today I am praying for...

PRAYER

Lord, help me to not lose my focus but instead keep my eyes trained on You, knowing You will provide for my needs. In Your holy name, Amen.

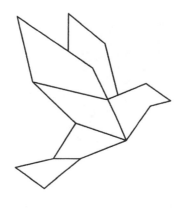

He will cover you with his feathers;
you will take refuge under his
wings. His faithfulness will be a
protective shield.

Psalm 91:4

DAY 18

Suppose the Worst

"Moses answered, 'What if they won't believe me and will not obey me but say, "The Lord did not appear to you"?' The Lord asked him, 'What is that in your hand?' 'A staff,' he replied" Exodus 4:1-2)

When it comes to carrying out God's will in our lives, do you suppose too much? Suppose we project potential, and ultimately invalid reasons, as to why God can't use us. Suppose you've done that before, how should you proceed? I'd like to encourage you to be emboldened by Moses' story of struggle. Moses supposed every possible negative; every reason why God's plan wouldn't work, even while he was speaking with the God of the universe (let that sink in). Talking to the One who doesn't suppose, because He doesn't need to, Moses almost "supposed" himself out of God's call.

Let's presume you are in the same boat as Moses, and you are supposing yourself out of God's plan. What do you need to know? Exactly this: If God has called, God will equip. Also, note that God doesn't need much to equip. In Moses' case, God used a stick. Isn't that great? Moses was feeling ill-prepared, so God reassured him by showing him what He could do with a basic

rod!

When God calls you (as He calls all of us), He will bestow upon you what you need. Suppose you don't have much, He can still use you; suppose you are weak and feel unusable, that's ok! All He needs is a simple stick. May we all stop supposing the worst, assuming we aren't qualified, and start listening and following His intentions and believing the best in our great God!

Written By Eric Souza

DAY 18
QUESTIONS

If God is calling you to step out in faith and do something, then how is He equipping you to succeed in that mission?

_____

_____

_____

_____

Today I praise God for...

_____

_____

_____

Today I am confessing...

_____

_____

_____

Today I am praying for...

_____

_____

_____

PRAYER

God, There are so many days when I think I know what's best. I know You must get tired of hearing me tell You how I think things should be. Help me to not suppose I know what's best anymore. Help me to seek Your will in all I do. In Jesus' name, Amen.

Trust in the Lord with all your heart, and do not rely on your own understanding; in all your ways know him, and he will make your paths straight.

Proverbs 3:5-6

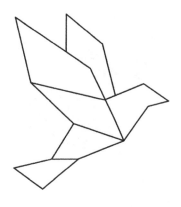

As you walk through the valley of the unknown, you will find the footprints of Jesus both in front of you and beside you.

- Charles Stanley

DAY 19

Cast Your Cares on the Lord

"Casting all your cares on him, because he cares about you"
1 Peter 5:7

Lately, it seems like awful news lurks in the world, our nations, sometimes within our own four walls. I know I'm supposed to cast my cares on the Lord, but sometimes these bad reports weigh me down. As I fumed over a personal problem while gardening, I spotted something strange. My lilies weren't blooming, they were all buds. Upon closer inspection, I noticed these nasty weeds were wrapping around the lily's stems. The weeds were pushing them on the ground. It seemed the weeds wanted to prevent the lilies from blooming.

While unraveling the weeds from the stems, I thought about how I can cast my cares on the Lord. Then I heard the Father speak to me in the midst of my garden! The Father told me I was letting the "weeds" of my life, the cares of this world, politics, saving money to support the long-term needs of my special needs son, were all dragging me down. These cares of life were blocking my calling, zapping my energy, and stealing God's destiny over my life.

Now, I realize I need to untangle my mind from worry and

truly cast my cares on Him. I had to trust Him with each of my problems. God knows exactly how to untangle each problem, since He's my Father, and He will take care of me for all of eternity.

So from now on, every time a care enters my mind, I'm casting the cares onto Him and focusing on His promises, His goodness, and His unconditional love.

Amazingly, overnight the freed lilies bloomed, illustrating how I will bloom as well when I truly cast my cares on Him.

Written By Susan Davis

DAY 19 QUESTIONS

What weeds in your life are choking you out? How can you go about unraveling their grip on your life so you can start blooming?

_____

_____

_____

_____

Today I praise God for...

_____

_____

Today I am confessing...

_____

_____

Today I am praying for...

_____

_____

_____

PRAYER

In Jesus' name help me cast all my cares upon You. Help me realize You care for me. Help me, Lord, not to let the weeds of life hold me down, and help me bloom into the destiny You have for me. Amen.

DAY 20

Persevere in the Unknown

"Set your minds on things above, not on earthly things"
Colossians 3:2

Do you think we can thrive in the face of uncertainty? Is there an action on our part that might make that a possibility? What does it take to persevere in the unknown? It takes focus! However, our focus must be on the right component. It can't be on us and our abilities. Nor can we only stare at our circumstances. Have you ever noticed the more we concentrate on our troubles, the more our despair increases? Our concentration needs a shift to something more significant. It isn't always easy. After all, we are human, and our thoughts sometimes feel uncontrollable. Yet, we all can choose to push the thoughts aside and focus on what will give us peace, joy, and the strength to persevere.

We must turn our focus to God. "Set your minds on things above, not on earthly things" (Colossians 3:2).

Have you ever had a child missing? You worry if they are cold and hungry or in danger. The fear of the unknown threatens to steal every ounce of energy you can muster up. You find yourself struggling to keep moving forward. Your mind becomes so cluttered with concern that making decisions and plans seems

impossible, yet your child needs you. I have been there, and the only way through it for me was to focus on God. Slowly but surely, as I turned my face towards Him, my worries turned into trust, and my mind was able to quiet enough to hear God's voice and plan. When we focus on God, it helps us embrace the unknown and thrive in the midst of it.

How else can we focus on God? Be present with the Lord. Sit at His feet daily. Push away all of the distractions and solely be with Him. Let this relationship be your most important one, especially when you can't see the next step to take. Listen carefully for what He might be asking; God loves to ask questions to help us find our way. Don't ever be afraid to inquire of Him. After all, questions help us to deepen relationships with others; why would it be any different with God? "Draw near to God, and he will draw near to you" (James 4:8).

It helps to remember what God has done in the past. Think about the times He answered your prayers or those of someone else. If you struggle to recall, start with the miracles in the Bible.

Practicing gratitude will turn our thoughts toward God's blessings and away from our circumstances. Also, it reminds us how much the Lord cares for us and the details of our lives. What are the blessings that come to your mind? "Rejoice always, pray constantly, give thanks in everything; for this is God's will for

DAY 20

you in Christ Jesus" (1 Thessalonians 5:16-18).

We need to strive for God's perspective. When we are fixated on what we think is right, we fail to see our situation from God's angle. Our vantage point is only a sliver of what God sees. He has the big picture in mind. We must shift our focus and seize what matters most to God. Love is definitely at the top, as demonstrated by Jesus over and over again. He commanded us to love one another. "This is my command: Love one another as I have loved you. No one has greater love than this: to lay down his life for his friends" John 15:12-13

Jesus took the time to connect with others. He frequently demonstrated how each person has value. Jesus never let the distractions or the busyness of life get in the way of spending time with His Father. Often in the Bible, we hear about Jesus removing Himself to a quiet place to commune with God. "Yet he often withdrew to deserted places and prayed" (Luke 5:16). Will you do the same? Consider what keeps you from focusing on God. Is it possible to eliminate some of those distractions? When we fill our minds with God's Word daily, it makes a difference. God speaks to us through His Word, and we don't want to miss His wisdom or comfort.

On more than one occasion, I have found myself dumbfounded by the results of reading His word. It is impressive

how the familiar stories we know suddenly give us a new message that speaks precisely to what we are going through. Most recently, it was the story of Noah. It seemed unthinkable that a man who built an ark could somehow speak to my current situation. One night, someone had judged me harshly for the unique way my marriage looked. After prayer and wise counsel my husband and I chose to live apart to help a hurting child. The words spoken rattled my mind but Noah gave me the courage to be obedient and keep my focus on God. After all, Noah had looked like a fool building a boat. However, despite any ridicule, he was obedient.

We all can endure the unknown to some degree. However, don't you want to do more than get through your difficult circumstances? Don't you want to thrive and persevere in the unknown? The number one way is to focus on God. Of course, it won't wipe away the pain or frustration. However, when we focus on God, we will gain His wisdom, strength, and hope. But best of all, we will never be alone.

Written By Maree Dee

DAY 20
QUESTIONS

If your focus is on the unknown, what steps can you take to shift your thoughts and perspective to God?

_____

_____

_____

_____

Today I praise God for...

_____

_____

_____

Today I am confessing...

_____

_____

_____

Today I am praying for...

_____

_____

_____

PRAYER

Most holy Lord, help me to keep my mind and heart focused on You! Amen.

DAY 21

Be Still and Know That I Am God

"Stop fighting, and know that I am God, exalted among the nations, exalted on the earth" Psalm 46:10

"God is our refuge and strength, a helper who is always found in times of trouble. Therefore we will not be afraid, though the earth trembles and the mountains topple into the depths of the seas, though its water roars and foams and the mountains quake with its turmoil…'Stop fighting, and know that I am God, exalted among the nations, exalted on the earth.' The Lord of Armies is with us; the God of Jacob is our stronghold'" (Psalm 46:1-3, 10-11).

As I wrote this the world was experiencing a pandemic. Everything seemed unsettled and the future cloudy. People's lives had been upended. Many contracted COVID-19 and thousands died. Even more were impacted by the economic and social consequences of trying to minimize the spread of this virus. There are likely very few people today who were not touched in one way or another, either directly or indirectly, by this disease. People's responses to COVID-19 covered a wide spectrum. Some denied it was that bad. At the other extreme were those who said it would cause a major shift in the way we live; a new normal. There were those who saw it as a government plot to gain more

power over ordinary citizens. Others saw it as God's judgment on a humanity that had turned away from Him. Many simply wanted it to go away so they could get back to work, be with family and friends, or whatever else they were being kept from.

Without question, this virus disrupted lives across the globe. But it provided us with an opportunity as well. Our lives leaned toward being busy. Between work, family obligations, church, social commitments, and endless entertainment and recreational opportunities, our lives are full. We have grown accustomed to having every moment of our waking lives filled with something. But that comes at a cost.

When my life is so full, it is hard to find time to fit God into my schedule. All too often we satisfy ourselves with a couple of hours on Sunday and maybe some other activity during the week. But do we ever slow down enough to just sit at Jesus' feet for a while? To enjoy His presence and get to know Him better? When your life is put on hold what will you do with that time? Will you fill it with meaningless activities? Or will you take advantage of the opportunity to simply be still and know God?

I would encourage you to do the latter. Join with the psalmist in turning away from fear and anxiety. Know that God is our refuge and strength, an ever-present help in our troubles. Respond to His invitation to be still and know that

DAY 21

He is God. Turn off the TV. Put down the book. Stop whatever you have been doing to fill your time. Find a quiet, solitary, and comfortable location. Still the voices that fill the emptiness. Just meditate on who God is and what He has done for you. It will be hard at first. But I promise that if you persist, you will find it well worth your time. Please do not let this opportunity pass you by.

Written By Ed Jarrett

DAY 21
QUESTIONS

What can you do to preserve the "slowdown" that came with COVID in 2020 so that you can continue to focus your time and attention more on God and prevent anxiety?

_____

_____

_____

Today I praise God for...

_____

_____

_____

Today I am confessing...

_____

_____

_____

Today I am praying for...

_____

_____

_____

_____

PRAYER

Lord, my life gets so busy. If necessary, take away the things that fill up every moment of my day. Give me a desire to spend more time alone with You. In Your precious name, Amen.

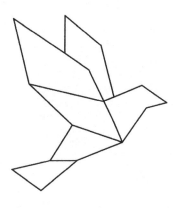

When I am afraid,
I will trust in you.
Psalm 56:3

DAY 22

Trust in the Lord

"The person who trusts in the Lord, whose confidence indeed is the Lord, is blessed" Jeremiah 17:7

Trusting in the Lord is so important, but sometimes so difficult. You love the Lord and you are thankful for every single blessing He has chosen to bestow upon you. But what do you do when you are going through hard times and you have prayed and all you seem to hear from God is silence? How do you hold on to your faith in such circumstances?

Sometimes we feel we must do things on our own. We focus so much energy on finding the way ourselves, that our minds become confused and our faith begins to waver. We know we must do the work, but we must have trust and faith that God will not only show us in which direction to go, but He will have our rewards waiting for us when we get there, thanks to His grace and mercy.

So how do we achieve this? How can we make sense of all that is going on in our lives, and still trust in the Lord to handle it? First, we must give it to God, laying all our fears and worries and problems at His feet. Try not to think of this as a difficult task. In fact, that's actually the easy part. The hard part is not picking it

back up.

That is the second thing. So many times we will go to God in prayer and truly empty ourselves of all the pain and anxiety we are going through, but the next day we find ourselves, once again, worrying about those same problems. Why would we worry if we truly gave it to God because faith shows us it will be taken care of? We can't do any of it alone, but only through true faith and trust in the Lord, can we accomplish these goals.

"'For I know the plans I have for you'—this is the Lord's declaration—'plans for your well-being, not for disaster, to give you a future and a hope'" (Jeremiah 29:11).

God has such a beautiful plan for our lives. Isn't it about time we allow Him to reveal the plans He has for each of us, so that we may flourish in rich, new lives, grounded in Christ Jesus?

Written By Gina Barton Sewell

PRAYER

Father God, thank You so much for Your grace and mercy. Thank You for loving us so much that You sent Your Son to die on the cross for us. The Bible tells us that You will never leave, nor forsake us, and that is such a beautiful promise a promise that can carry us through tough times. We need only to trust in You Lord. In Jesus' name, Amen.

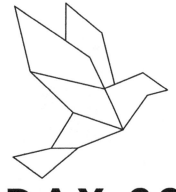

DAY 22
QUESTIONS

In what area of your life have you prayed and released to God only to pick that burden back up again? Why do you keep doing this and how can you stop?

Today I praise God for...

Today I am confessing...

Today I am praying for...

DAY 23

Keeping Our Eyes on Jesus

"Therefore, since we also have such a large cloud of witnesses surrounding us, let us lay aside every hindrance and the sin that so easily ensnares us. Let us run with endurance the race that lies before us, keeping our eyes on Jesus, the pioneer and perfecter of our faith. For the joy that lay before him, he endured the cross, despising the shame, and sat down at the right hand of the throne of God" Hebrews 12:1-2

Have you ever experienced something that shook your faith? Something that happened so quickly yet was out of your control? When these events happen, our human nature has a hard time keeping our eyes on Jesus, but we can learn to trust Him through these events.

My daughter was almost run over. It wasn't her fault, but maybe I should start at the beginning. It started out like any other day. We ran through our morning routine, which ended up in the drop-off lane at school. We were running a touch behind schedule, so it was backed up. Thus, I pulled into the far lane, which isn't abnormal. I reminded the girls to watch for cars, told them I loved them and watched them cross over the lanes. Traffic was at a standstill. The truck in the front of the first lane

was letting his child out, so my daughter started to cross in front of him. But as soon as his child shut the door, he started to pull out. He didn't even look. At that moment, my heart stopped. It was over in an instant. He quickly slammed on the breaks. My daughter gave him a deer-in-the-headlights kind of look and then finished crossing the drop-off zone.

It was over. Only it wasn't. I made it halfway home before I burst into tears. When talking to my husband about it, he said we should focus on how good God is — on what a blessing it was that the driver saw her before it was too late. He said we should be thankful this experience would stick with her and help her to be more aware of her surroundings. Yet the momma in me just wanted to hold her close and cry. It's so easy to get stuck in that moment.

Have you ever been there? Have you ever found yourself in a moment like that? Where the event is over, yet the fear is still gripping your heart? You're afraid of what might have been? Or maybe it's anger? Sometimes something happens, and it really gets under my skin. Even though it really shouldn't. It's something that happened in a moment and it's over. Yet I'm still seething. In moments like those, I'm thankful for my husband. He always listens to my side of the story, gently reminds me that God is good and that I should act like it. Usually, in just the

DAY 23

words I need to hear.

In the book of Hebrews, Paul wrote, "Therefore, since we also have such a large cloud of witnesses surrounding us, let us lay aside every hindrance and the sin that so easily ensnares us. Let us run with endurance the race that lies before us, keeping our eyes on Jesus, the pioneer and perfecter of our faith. For the joy that lay before him, he endured the cross, despising the shame, and sat down at the right hand of the throne of God" (Hebrews 12:1-2). That's where I mess up. I take my eyes off Jesus. Instead of running the race God has set out for me, I'm shaken and fixated on an event in the past. I'm stuck on a moment and even though nothing bad happened in that moment, I let it trip me up anyway. I let it slow me down. I don't know if that's something you can relate to or not, but I know this isn't a one-time thing for me. However, it's something that I can work on now that I'm aware of it. In fact, now that I'm aware of it, I can recognize it as a sin that so easily trips me up. And if it's a struggle you share, maybe you can too.

Written By Heather Hart

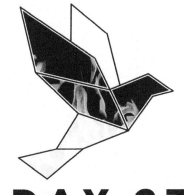

DAY 23
QUESTIONS

In what area of your life do you hold on to fears that should be released to God?

Today I praise God for...

Today I am confessing...

Today I am praying for...

PRAYER

Lord, so often I can't see past the bad things, the things that don't matter. Help me keep on running my race and see what You want me to see. Amen.

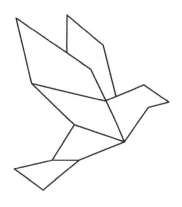

Where does your security lie? Is God your refuge, your hiding place, your stronghold, your shepherd, your counselor, your friend, your redeemer, your saviour, your guide? If He is, you don't need to search any further for security.
- Elisabeth Elliot

DAY 24

Repressing Fear

"I have told you these things so that in me you may have peace. You will have suffering in this world. Be courageous! I have conquered the world" John 16:33

Fear. It seems to be the topic of so many discussions lately. Honestly, I'm kind of tired of it. You ever heard the phrase, "There's nothing to fear but fear itself"? Yup. I think that's where so many of us are. We can hardly leave our homes any more without being scared of something.

We might get in an accident. Or worse yet, our kids might get in an accident when they drive away in the car alone for the first time. Someone might come into the store where we're shopping and start shooting. You "can't" use your key fob to lock your car doors because someone might be nearby stealing the "code" so they can rob you while you're running your errand. We might bump into someone who's sick and catch whatever they have, whether it be the flu or bed bugs.

Doesn't this seem a bit ridiculous? Do you ever stop to think who is behind all the fear-mongering that is so prevalent in today's society? Believe it or not, it isn't the government or even the media. It's Satan himself. Fear doesn't come from God.

"The fear of mankind is a snare, but the one who trusts in the Lord is protected" (Proverbs 29:25).

I'm certainly not against being prepared. We have life insurance policies to make sure loved ones are taken care of when we do die. But we don't live each day in anticipation of dying. Being prepared is different than panicking and being scared at what's around every corner. That is not how God would have us live our lives. We can't let fear overtake us.

In these times of stress and panic, be the one who helps to calm others' spirits. Be the voice of reason. Pray with someone if need be. Maybe it's time they accepted Christ as their Savior so they can be assured of their final destination.

There's another phrase that's popular today. "Keep calm and carry on." Maybe that is the one we need to be taking to heart. Be calm. Don't fear.

The next time you feel fear and anxiety rising in your heart, take a deep breath and pray. Close your eyes and imagine holding your open hands out to God (or you could physically hold out your hands) and giving Him all your concerns. Give it all to Him and let Him take care of whatever it is that stirs up your anxious heart.

Written By Ruth O'Neil

PRAYER

Lord, You know that Satan tries to deceive us every single day to keep us living in fear of everything. Calm our spirits. Be with us. Give us comfort even in the darkest of days. Amen.

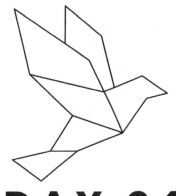

DAY 24
QUESTIONS

What thing(s) steal your joy and keep you from being calm? Why do they do that and how can you combat that fear?

_____

_____

_____

_____

Today I praise God for...

_____

_____

_____

Today I am confessing...

_____

_____

_____

Today I am praying for...

_____

_____

_____

_____

DAY 25

A Front Row Seat
to the Unthinkable

I will lead the blind by a way they did not know; I will guide
them on paths they have not known. I will turn darkness to
light in front of them and rough places into level ground.
This is what I will do for them, and I will not abandon them.
Isaiah 42:16

"What is your biggest fear?"

I had a couple of minutes to think as other guests on the
panel answered the question. What will I say? I'm not a good
swimmer, so deep water is on the list. Hiking in the mountains
and confronting a snake is another. I know my limits in a lake or
ocean, and hiking is a rare activity, so neither of those answers is
realistic. This was not the time to be clever. I needed to answer
honestly.

"My biggest fear is losing my husband and living alone."

Several years later, I had a front row seat to that event. Two
thousand miles from home, and two days before Christmas,
my husband suffered a fatal heart attack. I was numb and
heartbroken, but surprisingly, despite my anticipated fear, not
afraid. My new path of widowhood held unfamiliarity. Confusion

144

and discouragement wove threads with learning new skills. Although I had anticipated fear, that thread never surfaced in the fabric of my widowhood.

Years earlier, my daughter and her husband selected a verse for their marriage:

"I will lead the blind by a way they did not know; I will guide them on paths they have not known. I will turn darkness to light in front of them and rough places into level ground. This is what I will do for them, and I will not abandon them." (Isaiah 42:16)

Jon and Susan looked at marriage in their early twenties as an unfamiliar path. Now I, married for forty-two years, faced a life-changing path marked with singleness. In reversed roles, I had never done this before either. I pulled out that verse and clung to key words and phrases for security:

- I: (God who knows and loves me.)
- Will lead: (That's declarative, not tentative.)
- Blind: (I've never seen this life path before.)
- Unfamiliar: (I've never traveled the "I" and "mine", only the "we" and "ours".)
- I will: (God is determined, not maybe or if it's convenient.)
- Guide: (Direction from One who knows the path well.)
- Darkness into light: (He gives me a lamp and light for the step I'm on.)

DAY 25

- Rough to level: (It's difficult but will get easier and more stable.)
- This is what I will do for them, and I will not abandon them. (It's repeated so I understand God means it. He will be my companion.)

As I walked in loss and loneliness, I met challenges and dilemmas. In each new season, I was traveling an unfamiliar and unknown path. Uncertainties, adjustments, and major decisions were written in my calendar.

But I did not meet fear. I thought I would. I had thought about it for years. I answered that question during a panel discussion, but fear did not surface.

What did surface? God's faithfulness and promises.

Just as He promised to lead and accompany me along the most unfamiliar and emotional path of my life, He reminded me of other promises.

I learned each day His unfailing love and personal mercies for my uncertain and difficult steps keep me from falling apart. "Because of the Lord's faithful love we do not perish, for his mercies never end" (Lam. 3:22).

I learned I can rely on His trustworthy presence, and He knows every detail of my life. "You have encircled me; you have placed your hand on me" (Psalm 139:5a).

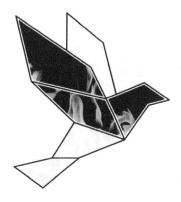

And in those hard times, when my eyes were filled with tears, He spoke, "But he said to me, 'My grace is sufficient for you, for my power is perfected in weakness'" (2 Corinthians 12:9a).

Reflecting on my answer that day, the unthinkable did happen. My husband died suddenly, and I am a widow and alone. But my anticipated response didn't happen. I don't live in fear. My other responses to cling to the truths of God's guidance, love, and faithfulness that cover fear made the difference.

What are you facing today—an imagined fear, or the reality of a hardship with more questions than answers? You may be walking a life-altering experience and question if you can even get up. Those same promises are for you as well. There is One who will help you rise to your feet and hold your hand for the next step.

"For I am the Lord your God, who holds your right hand, who says to you, 'Do not fear, I will help you'" (Isaiah 41:13).

Life altering events happen and problems remain, but so does God's presence—all that He is and all that He promises.

Written By Marilyn Nutter

DAY 25
QUESTIONS

As you name your fears, what scriptures can you put against your fears to make them powerless?

_____
_____
_____
_____

Today I praise God for...

_____
_____
_____

Today I am confessing...

_____
_____
_____

Today I am praying for...

_____
_____
_____

PRAYER

Father, I am so limited in my thinking and responses to difficult times. I often place fear instead of You, front and center. Help me to cling to Your promises, that You will guide me faithfully for the next step, and that your grace and love are present to remove my anxiety and fear. In Jesus' name, Amen.

DAY 26

Fears In All Sizes

"But whoever listens to me will live securely and be undisturbed by the dread of danger." Proverbs 1:33

In the course of my lifetime, I have had legitimate fears that lead to anxiety. I call them legitimate because of the magnitude. For example:

- When one of my children was injured or sick
- When I feared for my daughter's life
- When someone broke into my house in the middle of the night
- When my dad had Alzheimer's disease

Yes, these, along with many others not listed, seem like good reasons to fear. They certainly robbed me of sleep. Then my granddaughter told me her fear. She said, "Grandma, my future looks non-existent with global warming and pollution." She did not even mention wars and biological warfare, but her words made me very sad. Her fears are genuine. I also watch in horror on the news those trying to escape hostile areas. Those fears are almost more than I can comprehend.

Yet as a Christian, I must ask myself, "Are any fears truly legitimate when I have the power of the Creator of the Universe

on my side?" When I reveal them in the light of God Almighty, all my fears, even monumental ones, may resemble my minor fear of roaches — silly!

I have never liked roaches, but when we moved down south, the definition of a roach reached a whole new level. First of all, these bugs are so much bigger than they are up north. One looks almost like a tiny mouse. Second, they fly. Merely explaining it makes me shiver! As a child, an emergency trip to the doctor after a bug flew into my ear gave me an everlasting fear of bugs that fly. Now just let that sink in — it's like a little flying mouse! Third, I had run-ins with roaches. I had one in my shoe while putting it on. I had two separate occasions when one of these creatures got on me in restaurants. And the worst was when one tried to get in my mouth during the night while sleeping. Ugh!

I confess. I have a fear of roaches. I literally scream when I see one, and let me tell you, that's not good in a restaurant.

I remember a time when I was about to perform a piano concert. I had the jitters, and my heart started pounding in my chest. I stopped what I was doing, bowed my head, and went to God in prayer. I asked, "Dear Lord, I'm ready to play the piano, but I am nervous. Would you please take away these nerves and replace them with your peace? I ask for my hands to be yours and for you to play in my place. If I play well or poorly, it's up to

DAY 26

you. Thank you." I took a deep breath and instantly felt a peace that passed all understanding. My hands played that piano by the power of God. It was glorious, and I will never forget it.

So, if I can tap the power of God, what is my problem? I believe it all has to do with my spiritual faith application. I don't always release myself and let God fully take over my life. By the power of Jesus, I should be able to move mountains, yet when I have a minor obstacle, like a roach, and I ask God, why can't I get rid of it? He answers:

"Because of your little faith. . .For truly I tell you, if you have faith the size of a mustard seed, you will tell this mountain, 'Move from here to there,' and it will move. Nothing will be impossible for you." Matthew 17:20

Nothing is impossible tells me that no fear is legitimate, not a big one or a small one. With my faith in Jesus, significant problems are no problems to Him. So, the linchpin is faith, and since faith comes from God, all I need to do is ask. He loves me so much that he won't give me a scorpion if I ask for bread. If I ask for faith, He will answer.

Corrie ten Boom, the author of "The Hiding Place," tells the story of how she lived through the horrors of a Nazi concentration camp. She knew deep sorrow, suffering, and pain. She could have had legitimate reasons to be afraid, yet a quote

by Corrie was, "When a train goes through a tunnel, and it gets dark, you don't throw away the ticket and jump off. You sit still and trust the engineer." Even amid a deplorable situation, Corrie sat still and placed her complete faith in her Supreme Engineer — God!

Faith brings us to a closer relationship with God. In the end, that is His deep desire for us. When we are close to Him, we can hear as He whispers in our ears.

"But whoever listens to me will live securely and be undisturbed by the dread of danger." (Proverbs 1:33)

Crises come in all sizes. So do fears. God may not remove the danger, but He definitely can eradicate our dread. Our omnipotent Father is superior to all our anxieties, whether monumental, like life or death, or insignificant, like a roach. By the power of the faith God gives us, His peace will obliterate any fear.

Written By Jenny Calvert

DAY 26
QUESTIONS

What is keeping you from a closer relationship with the one who gives sweet peace?

Today I praise God for...

Today I am confessing...

Today I am praying for...

PRAYER

Dearest Father, Please help me to listen to your voice intently. I ask for more faith to be closer to you, knowing that in your secure presence, I need not fear. Amen.

DAY 27

Peace in the Night

"I will both lie down and sleep in peace, for you alone, Lord, make me live in safety." Psalm 4:8

Her eyes are wild with fear; her body rigid. She tries to speak but the words won't come, only guttural noises from somewhere deep inside. Instinctively, I reach for her, but she lurches away from me, bristling like a cornered animal, frantically clawing her way free from some unseen yet clearly terrifying threat. As her mom, I am reduced to the role of helpless bystander, simply watching over her until her breathing slows, her heart rate regulates, and peace is finally restored to her anxious, restless mind.

The psalmist in Psalm 91:5 tells us with authority, "You will not fear the terror of the night." And yet, so often I do. I have seen the way it manifests in the semi-conscious, animalistic behavior of my 6-year-old daughter. And I have experienced how it infiltrates the sanctuary and security of my sleep, too.

I may not suffer from night terrors myself, but I have found that in the silence and darkness of the night—alone, without distractions—my mind is vulnerable to attack and my anxious thoughts are prone to spiral. Little seeds of worry, doubt, and

fear sprout into giant stalks before my eyes, crowding out my peace of mind until, before I know it, my palms are sweaty, my breathing is rapid, and my thoughts are circling the drain of panic, helplessness, and despair.

King David most likely knew what it felt like to face an anxious night, spending years on the run from the enemies who so relentlessly pursued him. And yet, still, he was able to put the terrors of the night to rest and say with confidence, "I will both lie down and sleep in peace" (Psalm 4:8a).

How is this possible? The second half of the verse gives us the answer:

"...for you alone Lord, make me dwell in safety."

The source of David's peace was God alone. He wasn't lying awake worrying—as I so often am—desperately searching for solutions to all his problems or analyzing every possible worst-case scenario. No, David trusted fully in God for his safety and protection, having full assurance that as one of God's faithful people, his prayers had been heard (Psalm 4:3) and that God would deliver him from his current affliction as He had many times before (Psalm 4:1). As he wrote in Psalm 34:4-5, "I sought the Lord, and he answered me and rescued me from all my fears. Those who look to him are radiant with joy." While others around him found joy in material things, David's joy and ultimate

DAY 27

hope remained in the Lord (Psalm 4:7), and in surrendering his situation to the only One who was sovereign over his circumstances. No matter how insurmountable they may have seemed, David was able to sleep peacefully and find true rest.

When we fix our minds on worldly things, our anxious thoughts can be overwhelming. But, like David, when we focus on God alone, peace will surely follow. Isaiah 26:3 says: "You will keep the mind that is dependent on you in perfect peace, for it is trusting in you." Jesus even tells us in John 14:27: "Peace I leave with you. My peace I give to you...Don't let your heart be troubled or fearful."

As believers, this gift of peace is ours for the taking. We need only to remember where to look for it and, more importantly, who to ask for it.

When the terrors of the night inevitably threaten our peace of mind, we can not only fix our eyes on Jesus, the true source of our peace, but also cast the weight of our burdens onto His shoulders (1 Peter 5:7). He is no helpless bystander but is willing and able to carry them — all the way to the cross. For only there do we have the final victory over the enemy and his insidious attacks on our mind, and gain an eternal perspective through which every anxious, fearful thought finds its proper place.

Written By Vicki Bentley

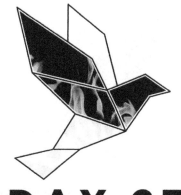

DAY 27
QUESTIONS

When the terrors of the night disturb your peace, where do you turn? In those moments, how can you more intentionally focus your attention on God instead of your circumstances?

Today I praise God for...

Today I am confessing...

Today I am praying for...

PRAYER

Father God, thank You that we need not fear the terrors of the night, and can instead lie down and sleep in peace knowing You are Sovereign over all our circumstances and the only true Source of our peace, joy, and hope. When anxiety strikes, help us fix our eyes on You alone, trusting in Your faithfulness and protection, and surrendering every last fear into Your capable hands. Amen.

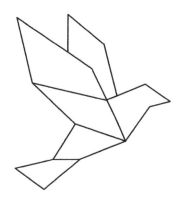

Come to me, all of you who are weary and burdened, and I will give you rest.

Matthew 11:28

DAY 28

How Meditation Quells Fear

"The Lord is my rock, my fortress, and my deliverer, my God, my rock where I seek refuge, my shield and the horn of my salvation, my stronghold." Psalm 18:2

I clung to this verse like a rock climber one year. No, I've never climbed an actual rock wall, but I'm glad God's Word was like a steady rock in my turmoil.

That year, I was seven months pregnant with my third child. My work contract was in legal debate. When I went in for prenatal checkups, my doctor looked at my spiking numbers and asked if I was facing unusual stress. That was an understatement.

My lawyer had counseled me to either keep working under the less-than-perfect conditions or quit. There was no wiggle room in the contract.

I was soon to be a mom of a 4-year-old, a 2-year-old, and a newborn. The one big perk of my job was being able to work from home. I didn't want to go out and find another job to leave them in another's care. I wanted to be the best mom I could be, and that looked like staying home with them.

However, our finances were tight. We really couldn't afford for me to quit. But I hated working for people who seemed just

like the enemies David described in Psalm 18.

Between more (expensive) meetings with my attorney and stressful conversations with my husband, I experienced premature contractions at week 36. The doctor put me on bed rest, and my schedule skidded to a halt.

I couldn't accomplish much in that state. But I could read and pray instead of worrying all day. So, I kept my Bible open to Psalm 18, meditating on the truths every time my anxiety rose. The names of God in verse 2 became secure places on which I could rest my faith.

- My rock – he is immovable, impenetrable, solid.
- My fortress – where I could go for safety and security.
- My deliverer – the only one who could lift me out of my pit.
- My refuge – a quiet place in my chaos.
- My shield – the one who protected me in the real, yet unseen, spiritual battle.
- The horn of my salvation – The only one who could save and rescue me. The one I could hold onto when I felt afraid.
- My stronghold – My bunker against the coming storms.

Meditating on these truths about God's unchanging character helped me cling to truth in my trial. They were a steady place

DAY 28

to land when my thoughts wanted to run wild. I knew that I wouldn't be in that trap forever, and God would carry me through to the other side. He was already waiting for me there.

My fears that year seemed sky high. Yet meditating on the names of God in Psalm 18 truly brought me the peace I was seeking. He became ever more personal and caring to me in that difficult time. As I look back today, I thank God for giving me that psalm when I needed it. He taught me to meditate on it to quell my fears, and I'm certain he wants you to do the same, friend.

Written By Sarah Geringer

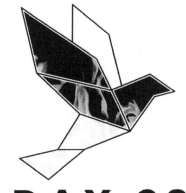

DAY 28
QUESTIONS

How can meditating on God's names quell the fears you are facing now?

Today I praise God for...

Today I am confessing...

Today I am praying for...

PRAYER

Father, I praise you as my rock, my refuge, my stronghold in times of trouble. When I am afraid, help me put my trust in you as I meditate on the truths in your Word. Help me cling to your character like I would cling to a wall as a rock-climber. I believe that you will carry me through this valley and meet me on the other side. In Jesus' name, Amen.

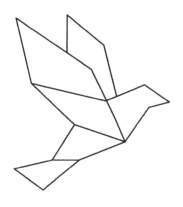

And if the Spirit of him who raised Jesus from the dead lives in you, then he who raised Christ from the dead will also bring your mortal bodies to life through his Spirit who lives in you.

Romans 8:11

DAY 29

Trapped by a Difficult Problem

"Because he has his heart set on me, I will deliver him; I will protect him because he knows my name." Psalm 91:14

When I walked into my living room one morning last summer, I noticed my two cats behaving unusually. Standing on their hind legs, they had their front paws propped up on the cold metal rim of the wood stove door and were staring intently through the glass-plated door into the dim interior. Wondering what could possibly have them so enthralled, I joined them in peering into the stove. There, I saw a small bird fluttering in the ashes. Somehow the bird had fallen down the stove pipe and, because the chimney is so narrow, it was unable to fly back out. Despite its efforts to escape, it was hopelessly trapped. Moved with compassion for its plight, I set out on a mission to liberate it.

After locking my cats in a separate room, I opened all the doors and windows in my living room to give the bird plenty of exit points. Then, I carefully unsealed the wood stove door. Hungry for fresh air and open skies, the little bird rocketed out of the stove and straight out the back door, a little dusty but otherwise unharmed.

Sometimes in life, I feel like that bird — trapped by my

problems with no discernible way out. Try as I might, I can't untangle the trouble myself. When those times come and I'm tempted to become discouraged, I like to remind myself that what seems impossible from my point of view is easily solvable from God's perspective. He sees the doors that I can't see, and He knows the perfect time to open them.

How about you? Do you feel trapped by a difficult problem? Perhaps you have a medical problem, a legal problem, or a relationship problem that feels insurmountable. Perhaps you've turned to the left and you've turned to the right, and there is no solution in sight. If so, find hope and comfort in the words of God found in Psalm 91:14: "Because he has his heart set on me, I will deliver him; I will protect him because he knows my name."

No matter how impossible your situation seems, God can make a way where there seems to be no way. While you wait for Him to rescue you, focus on loving Him and trusting Him. Hold fast to Him, and wait patiently for His deliverance. Just like the door eventually opened for my little bird, the door to freedom will open for you too.

Written By Carina Alanson

DAY 29
QUESTIONS

What situation in your life right now requires a perspective shift that only God can show?

Today I praise God for...

Today I am confessing...

Today I am praying for...

PRAYER

Lord, so often I want to do things in my own strength, but I fail. I need You to lift me up and carry me through the difficult days that come my way. Help me never to forget that my help comes from You. In your holy name, Amen.

DAY 30

Heart of Worship

"Enter his gates with thanksgiving and his courts with praise. Give thanks to him and bless his name. For the Lord is good, and his faithful love endures forever; his faithfulness, through all generations." Psalm 100:4-5

David had everlasting joy that comes only from the presence of God—the joy that defeated his anxiety in his worst moments.

When we give our lives to Jesus, we inherit that same joy. We are now set apart by God through the Holy Spirit. But, oh, how we must constantly guard our heart and joy from the enemy, especially in our darkest seasons. In those times, Satan will prey on our weaknesses and create anxiety and chaos in our thoughts. The longer we entertain these thoughts, the greater anxiety grows within us. We cannot have the peace of God without the presence of God. To live in joy means to live in the presence of God. He is not an object we put on a shelf and take down when we need something. He is our constant source of life and joy.

In Psalm 100, David tells us to acknowledge the Lord is God. We should accept His authority over every detail of our life. Worship and prayer are supposed to be life-long acts of the born-again believer.

We were designed with a heart and desire to worship the one true God; the Lord of Lords and the King of Kings. When we exalt Christ in every area of our life, every day of our life, we are weeding out anxiety while cultivating a lifestyle of worship. Moreover, as we are entering His gates daily with praise and thanksgiving for His enduring love and direction, our focus is on Him and others, not on ourselves. Our anxieties are replaced with peace.

Our worship can expound further into our life as we love others — helping and encouraging them in their time of need. When we serve others, we are reflecting the light of Jesus and exalting God.

I want to encourage you to find solace in the Word of God and through worship and prayer to God. No matter what you are going through, what stage of life you are in, you can find direction and peace within His Word and through prayer. If times are good, give praise to God, and thank Him for those times. Reflect on how He helped you through the bad times and give Him praise.

If you are going through a trial right now, pray. Talk to God. He wants to hear it all and He will see you through it all. We will run into roadblocks in life, but it does not mean we will never reach our destination. Sometimes the detours are blessed

DAY 30

diversions as the destination is prepared with extra amenities especially designed for us by God. While a heart of misery will breed anxiety when the path becomes bumpy, a heart filled with the joy of the Lord will delight in the sights along the way, knowing the destination will be worth all the discomforts.

Is your road rocky and broken? You do not have to travel alone; Jesus is ready and waiting to take you on the best ride of your life.

I hope you find peace and joy in the Lord today.

God is good all the time. And all the time, God is good. We should be giving Him honor, praise and glory all the time.

Written By Crystal Dixon

DAY 30
QUESTIONS

If the road you are traveling has taken a detour, perhaps for the worse, how can you quell your anxiety by knowing God is in control and guiding your journey?

Today I praise God for...

Today I am confessing...

Today I am praying for...

PRAYER

Thank you, Father, for your Son, Jesus. Thank you, Jesus, for dying on the cross so that we can have everlasting life. Thank you, Holy Spirit, for filling us with Your joy, casting out anxiety, and guiding our paths. May we have hearts of prayer and worship for You, Father, Our God. In Jesus' name. Amen

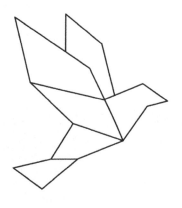

This is the word of the Lord

your Maker, the one who formed

you from the womb:

He will help you.

Do not fear, Jacob my servant,

Jeshurun whom I have chosen.

Isaiah 44:2

ABOUT THE AUTHORS

Alexis Newlin

Alexis is a 38-year-old lover of Jesus, loose leaf tea, roller coasters, writing stories, and going on adventures.

authenticadventurescencal.com

Hadassah Treu

onthewaybg.com

Hadassah Treu is an award-winning Christian blogger, author, poet, and speaker, and the Encouraging Blogger Award Winner of 2020. She is passionate about encouraging people in the journey of faith and a deeper walk with God.

Kyle Chastain

Jesus at the center. I'm a husband and a daddy to two boys. Subscribe to my blog for more practical content that will help you build a faith that works.

kylechastain.com/subscribe

Erin Woodfin

Erin Woodfin served in Children's Ministry for 8 years and is currently a stay at home mom of 3 beautiful girls. Erin has a Masters in Christian Education from Southwestern Baptist Theological Seminary.

notonourwatchministries.com

lifeinthespaciousplace.wordpress.com

Lesley Crawford

Blogger, musician, and youth worker based in Scotland, exploring the spacious place with God.

Corbin Henderson

My name is Corbin Henderson. I am a student at Midwestern Baptist Theological Seminary and a pastor at the First Baptist Church of Ash Grove. I am married to the love of my life, Heaven.

agfirstbaptist.org

valerieriese.com

Valerie Riese

After suffering years of debilitating anxiety, Valerie learned that victory over anxiety comes only through surrender to Jesus. Valerie writes to point women to Jesus as co-director of Candidly Christian, and as a freelance devotional writer, proofreader, and editor.

ABOUT THE AUTHORS

Lori Schumaker

As a writer and speaker, Lori helps women make sense of God and His unconditional love for us. On her blog, she provides tools to help us grow in faith. She also contributes to several online publications and books, and is author of *Surrendered Hearts*.

lorischumaker.com

lynnchurchill.com

Lynn Churchill

I'm a freelance writer and child of God, simultaneously celebrating freedom in Christ while clinging madly to Him, and trying not to whine as He leads me along the narrow way.

Pamela Keener

Pamela is a daughter of the King, writer, speaker, and ministry leader. She has a passion for inspiring and encouraging women to seek Jesus in their daily lives.

pamelakeener.com

Donna E. Lane

Dr. Donna E. Lane is an award-winning author, professor, and Christian counselor. Her books include Seeking Treasures, Strength in Adversity, Wilderness Meditations, and Restored Christianity.

doctordlane.com

Melanie Makovsky

melaniemakovsky.com

My blog, From Eden's Dirt, is about finding hope through despair and faith through fear. I am called to walk alongside you on a path committed to trusting God through both joy and pain. I'm also a wife, a mother of 3, and a singer.

Jim Hughes

Jim has pastored several churches throughout his life and has worked many years in local factories to help support his family. The father of three married adult children, Jim has now authored many books.

cthroughmarriage.blogspot.com

Bryon Mondok

bryonmondok.com

Bryon Mondok is a digital engagement practitioner, mission's pastor, and former missionary. He loves to read, write, and run.

ABOUT THE AUTHORS

Jazmin Frank

Author, speaker, and Bible teacher. I help ordinary people love God and love His story.

jazminnfrank.com

word-strong.com

Trip Kimball

Teacher, writer, pastor, missionary, disciple-maker, mentor—I love Jesus, love my wife, children, grandkids, and the beach!

Beth Steffaniak

I'm a Christ-follower, wife, mother, life coach, and blogger at messymarriage.com. I love helping people grow closer in their relationship with God and others.

messymarriage.com

Eric Souza

Originally from Tucson, Arizona, Eric and his family moved to Jacksonville, Florida in 2012 to plant Reach Jax. Since planting the church, the Lord has stretched, challenged, changed, and blessed Eric. Much of his real-life experience is seen in his practical and biblical devotionals.

reachjax.com

susanldavis.com

Susan Davis

Susan is an ordained minister, blogger, aspiring author and special needs mom. She has been married for 28 years and resides in Illinois. Susan blogs about faith and prayer and offers free bible reading plans on her website.

Maree Dee

Maree Dee is a Writer | Speaker | Advocate | Ministry Leader – passionate about encouraging and equipping others to embrace life in the midst of the unexpected.

embracingtheunexpected.com

aclayjar.net

Ed Jarrett

I am a follower of Jesus, retired, married for 35 years, with 2 children, and 2 grandchildren. I enjoy gathering with the church, theology, reading, gardening, and backpacking.

ABOUT THE AUTHORS

Gina Barton Sewell

Gina Barton Sewell is a writer who lives in McKinney Texas with her husband, Spike. She has four sons and five grandchildren. She loves Jesus and she loves to write about him. She shares her journey in hopes to encourage others on her blog.

ginabartonsewell.com

AuthorHeatherHart.com

Heather Hart

"Heather is an award-winning author and member of the Association of Biblical Counselors. Her goal isn't to tell others how to do more, be better, or achieve perfection, it's to point them to Jesus."

Ruth O'Neil

Ruth O'Neil has been a freelance writer for more than 20 years, publishing hundreds of articles in dozens of publications. Ruth spends her spare time quilting, scrapbooking, and camping with her family.

amazon.com/Ruth-ONeil/e/
B00AJ5S3YQ

Marilyn Nutter

Marilyn Nutter is a contributor to compilations, online sites, and print publications. She is a facilitator for grief groups, a speaker, and Bible study leader.

MarilynNutter.com

Jenny Calvert

Jenny and her husband have five children and twelve grandchildren. She has a deep desire to promote the healing love of Christ for a hurting world.

facebook.com/adorajennycalvert

Vicki Bentley

A Scottish native, she currently lives in upstate New York with her family. As a published writer and editor, she especially loves to encourage women to pursue Jesus-centered, Spirit-led, joy-filled living in the trenches of motherhood.

vicki-bentley.com

Sarah Geringer

Sarah Geringer is a speaker, podcaster, artist and author of several books including *Transforming Your Thought Life: Christian Meditation in Focus*. She lives in southeast Missouri with her husband and three children.

sarahgeringer.com

ABOUT THE AUTHORS

Carina Alanson

Carina Alanson is a writer and course creator who is passionate about helping people live with purpose and grow in faith. For more encouragement and resources for purposeful living, visit her website.

carinaalanson.com

Crystal Dixon

crystaladixon.com

I am a messenger for Jesus, a wife, a step-mom, a Nana, and a daughter. My husband and I live in North Carolina. We have 2 daughters and 3 grandchildren. I split my work week between writing, teaching for a community colleges, and working in fashion.

JD Tyler

I'm a youth pastor and seminarian from Birmingham, Alabama. I love writing to help others find life and rest in Jesus.

jdtyler.co

Thank you so much for reading one of our devotional books. If you like what we're doing and want to read more, please take a look at our other devotional books and journals by visiting our website at https://devotableapp.com

If you like these types of books and devotionals, we'd love for you to take a look at our other journal and devotional *"Equality Created Equal in His Image"*.

We need to equip ourselves with the knowledge of God's word to combat the false teaching of racism, sexism, gender inequality, age discrimination, and other forms of bias that denies the rights God Himself has given to all humans.

In this devotional, let's learn about how we, as believers, are commanded to live out these truths of equality and diversity.

It features:

- 6x9 trim size with plenty of room to write
- An open journaling page at the end of each work for your reflections
- Guided questions each day helping you write about that week's devotion topic
- A beautiful layout growing with you as you journal through the week

Learn more about Devotable at devotableapp.com

Made in the USA
Monee, IL
11 December 2021

84803472R00103